Child of Baltimore

By

Tia L. Lincoln

ISBN: 1-4107-9820-8 (e-book)
ISBN: 1-4107-9819-4 (Paperback)

This book is printed on acid free paper.

1stBooks - rev. 09/27/03

The following story you are about to read is a work of nonfiction. It is all true based on my recollection of events and what has been told to me. Some names have been changed in order to protect the anonymity of those involved.
It was not easy reliving the past and facing the demons of my life in such a public manner. To all those who I have encountered and related to them the odd life I led and encouraged me to tell my story, this one is also for you.

This book is dedicated to my father, the funniest man I knew. Somehow you always knew how to make me laugh.

Acknowledgements

This book would not even be possible without the help and support of those closest to me. And in keeping it real, true Baltimore style, I have to list those names. First and foremost, I want to thank my husband for being there for me when I went through (and still am going through) all of my emotional changes during the investigation of my father's case. I know it wasn't easy living with me when my many mood swings led a lifestyle of their own. Thanks for being the man that you are.
Thanks to my friend, Katanya Williams because if it wasn't for your constant encouragement and faith in me, this book never would have been published. *Thanks for all those "late lunch breaks"!*
I want to thank my kids, for being "Mommy's Little Angels" and giving me all the quiet time I needed to write this book. You both mean more to me than my own life and every move I make, I make for you both. Thanks to all those challenging people I encountered who said I would fail in life and turned their backs on me. You've made me stronger and created a fighter in more ways than one. It's because of all your negativity that I found the courage to finally put these words in print.

Chapter One

This beginning part is for Daddy.

It was blustering cold on this February evening in 1995. The type of February where you are sick of all the snow, the rain, the ice. I snuggled up to my fiance, Jamal as we watched "Against the Wall" on HBO for the first time. Earlier in the evening, we made plans to visit my father at his new place on Northern Parkway on the East Side of Baltimore. It was to be a special visit since Jamal had never met my father and my father wanted to show off his new apartment that was closer to the suburbs of Towson, than any place he had ever lived before. I was proud of myself that year. Proud that I had a man that my father would be happy to meet. Proud that I would be getting married and settling down after a hectic life filled with regrets and bad choices. I was twenty-three that year but felt thirty-two. Young, but mature beyond my years, I looked forward to showing him how my life was now, how I would be living my life in the future. During the middle of the movie, I reluctantly called my mother for his new address and telephone number. I knew talking about him to her would only bring on a host of issues about why I should not be talking to him. When she found out that I would be visiting him tonight, she begins uttering excuses about why I shouldn't go.

She complained, "He probably don't even wanna see you after those games you ran on him the last time you saw him."

I said, "No, because remember when we went out to his job on Eastern Avenue? He said he wasn't even worried about that no more."

She continued to offer up excuses about why I shouldn't even visit him. After we chatted for another few minutes, I ended the conversation by telling her I would call him and see if he really wanted me out there or if he had other plans. When I called him, he was elated to hear from me. He was happy because he had finally moved off of Eager Street and out of the hood. He said, "I'm in a good neighborhood now. Yeah, bring him out here. I ain't seen you in so long! Don't come out here without Kendra."

After talking to him for a few minutes and assuring him that I was indeed coming out, I called my mother back again to let her know that I would be arriving soon to pick up my daughter, Kendra.

She continued to comment," You don't wanna go out there. You know he don't care nothin about y'all. He probably don't even remember Kendra. Ain't you even a little embarrassed to introduce Jamal to a junkie in the first place? He probably won't even remember that you was even coming."

The persuading went on and on.

After the movie, an ice storm began. The weather was vicious to say the least, but Jamal and I still looked forward to seeing my father. It was late, approximately eleven or so at night. We still had to

pick up my daughter from my mother's house in Owings Mills. From Northwest Baltimore, it usually takes about twenty five minutes to get to her house, but because of the icy weather, it took almost an hour. When I almost broke my neck on the ice walking back to the car, my mother asked me was I still going over to see him. I grudgingly agreed to go tomorrow. It was no longer even safe to drive and he lived completely on the other side of town. The streets were so bad because of the ice that some cars were pulling to the side of the road to wait out the storm.
I said, "Do you think I should at least call him and let him know that I probably will be coming over there tomorrow?"
She said, "No, he probably forgot you was even coming."
I buckled Kendra in her seat belt and informed Jamal that we probably should just go tomorrow when the weather was better. We headed home. I never even called him to let him know not to wait up for us, that I wasn't coming. If only I had called him, I would have learned that my brother and his best friend were already there with him. Not making that phone call would continue to haunt me for the next seven years.

The next evening, I was busy doing laundry in my basement. Jamal was working at his warehouse job in Owings Mills. I called my father when I woke up in the morning to see if it was okay if we visited today. I wanted to explain the reason why I didn't come the previous night was because of the ice storm. I called, but the phone just rang. I thought absolutely nothing of it and continued with my afternoon chores. I called at least three more times during the afternoon, but didn't get an answer. I thought maybe he stepped out or something. While I was folding clothes, I glanced over at the news at six. There was a major story about a Korean grocery storeowner who was shot to death in a robbery. His widow was on TV crying about how someone could do something so terrible in broad daylight. The police were still searching for the killer. *"That's nothing new in Baltimore City,"* I thought to myself as I continued folding the laundry. As I was contemplating this, the newscaster went into another story about another brutal killing in the 3500 block of East Northern Parkway. I tensed up for just a second to listen. The newscaster explained very little. But I do remember her mentioning that the *"victim"* was a former MTA bus driver who was in his mid to late forties. At that very moment while I was staring at the screen, my telephone rang. On the phone was my sister Cocoa. She told me that my other sister Poochie had just called her with some alarming news. She said that my father's friend, Herbert Ross, had just left her house crying that something awful had happened to our father. He said he had just come from his apartment, it was surrounded by cops. He complained that they wouldn't even let him in or near the place. I thought this was odd to say the least, but I informed them that I would find out just what the hell was going on. After I got off the phone with her, I called his number repeatedly. This time I let the phone ring at least twenty times. Still, no answer. Kind of worried now, I called Jamal at his job and told him that I think something has happened to my father or somebody in his house. Jamal's reply was, "It couldn't have been.

We were just supposed to meet him last night." I told him how I was repeatedly calling his number and nobody's answering. I told him about what I heard on the news and what I had heard from my sister. He calmed me down by telling me he probably just stepped out and "you know how your sisters are always exaggerating everything." He told me to keep calling to see if he would answer. I was kind of worried because I remember my father saying," I'm not going nowhere. I'm gonna be in this house until Tuesday." He was enjoying his vacation by relaxing and chillin at home. I pushed redial on my phone yet again. Finally, after at least thirty more rings, a strange voice answers with, "Yes?"
Surprised, I say," Can I speak to Leroy Lincoln?"
The "voice" asks," And who are you?"
I say, "This is his daughter Tia."
I remember, it was at that moment when my voice trembled with fear.
He said, "Well, I have to make sure you are who you say you are. What is your name again?"
I cut him off with," Can you just tell me if something happened to my father or not?"
He explained rather cordially, "I can not give out that information over the phone without knowing for sure exactly who you are."
I think it was at that moment when I knew that something horrible had happened. With the exception of a stillborn brother being buried when I was six, I had never experienced any kind of death in my family. No pets dying, no relatives. Nothing. I was totally not ready for this. In my mind, I told myself that whoever answered his phone somehow had it all wrong. Did

they even know for sure that if somebody was killed, hurt, or whatever, that it was even him? I thought they were absolutely mistaken.

The "voice" on the other end finally identified himself as Detective Carter from the Baltimore City Homicide Division. *"Homicide?"* I thought. It couldn't be. After I gave him my address and telephone number, he said he would be over to my home to explain what had happened. He still refused to even admit if my father was hurt, dead, or whatever. I couldn't even grasp the thought that my father was dead. *This is not possible*, I thought. I just talked to him last night. I remember soaking in my bathtub trying my best to tell myself that this could not be true. Maybe somebody else was killed over there and they *think* it's my father. But as I was telling myself this, I couldn't prevent the feeling of doom that was forming inside of me. I called Jamal and explained to him what happened on the phone with the detective. He said he was on his way home. I cried softly in spurts. *This cannot be happening*, I told myself. Totally not believing that he could be dead. *Please God don't let this be happening*. I called Cocoa back and told her the gist of my exchange with the detective. She was shocked, too. Detective Carter called me back to say that he would be over around eight to explain to me what was going on.

He asked," Are you in the house alone? Is there someone else with you?"

I told him that my fiance was on his way over. In the meantime, I tracked down a number for my mother's job that was to be used only in the case of an emergency. She was a domestic worker, a house cleaner. I hated to call her at work where the customer

was always home, but I had no choice. I felt that this would meet the criteria for an emergency, so I called.
"I think something happened to Daddy."
She asked," Why do you say that?"
I explained to her about the conversation with the detective, the story I heard on the news, and the conversation with my sister. I told her that the detective was coming over around eight to tell me for sure just what was going on. Calmly, she told me to let her know what he said when he came over. I completely swept it under the rug when she didn't act surprised, baffled, or anything. She seemed to be totally unconcerned.
When Detective Carter arrived along with his partner, they informed me right away that my father was indeed murdered in his own home. They couldn't even tell just yet whether he was shot, stabbed, or what. I completely lost it. I remember Jamal had to pick me up off the floor. I felt my heart cave in. I was never prepared for a death of this magnitude.
After I was somewhat composed, Detective Carter asked me if I knew anyone who would have any reason to murder my father. I said I didn't. I was just in so much shock. *"Why?"* I wondered. The detective left me his card in case I remembered anything that would be of some use to him. After they left, I cried some more. Then cried some more. I stayed downstairs on my couch for hours just crying and wondering who could have done this. When I called my mother back in tears and told her that this was indeed true, that he had been murdered, she had no response. She told me to call her back when she got home because she was busy on her job. I thought that was kind of strange, but

I waited for her to get home before I called her. When the smoke cleared and I calmed down for a bit, I tried to answer the question that the detective had asked me. *"Do you know anyone that could have done this?"* As much as I tried, I couldn't think of anybody who hated him more than my own mother. They were going through a nasty divorce after a twenty year marriage that was filled with everything from drug abuse to adultery. It was no secret that she detested him and she didn't hesitate to let this be known to anyone who would listen. Occasionally, she had even mentioned her desires of having him killed. But could she have had this done? She couldn't have, I thought. The thought just would not go away. I had to at least ask her. But before I did, I had to find out if I was just assuming things. I had to find out if I was the only one feeling this way. I got my other sisters on the phone. I called Marlene, Poochie, and Cocoa and had all of them on the phone at the same time. I informed them what had happened.

I asked, "Now I'm not going to put any crazy ideas in y'all head or nothing. I just want to ask y'all a question now that I have all of y'all on the phone at one time. The detective asked me who would hate Daddy enough to want to kill him. I'm not saying no names, but who do y'all think hates him enough to want him dead? Who do y'all think hates him more than anybody?"

Every last one of them said the same person. *Mama.* They were in shock just as I was, but I was compelled by something more. I was determined to find out who did this and why. If she didn't have anything to do with his murder, then I would find that out too. I was bound by my beliefs that some things are right and some things are wrong. I would do whatever in my ability to find out just what happened in that apartment on that icy night. I called my mother back after I got off the phone with them and flat out confronted her with it.

I asked, "Mama, you didn't have anything to do with this did you?"

Her response was," I can't believe every time something happens in this family, I'm always the one to blame! God, Leroy's not even buried yet and already y'all starting rumors about who it could be. He probably stole somebody's drugs or something. You know he was deep into that stuff."

I said, "I'm not blaming you, I'm just asking you. You did hate him and you did talk about having him killed, come to think of it."

She exclaimed," I just can't believe that you would think I had something to do with this."

We called the detectives again together to see if they had any other information they could give us as to what they thought had happened. Detective Carter told us that he was killed by blunt force trauma. That set off another wave of tears and pain because everyone had assumed that he had been shot. Not only was he murdered, but he was brutally murdered with his brains splattered everywhere. (Even when we tried to retrieve his things the next day, the landlord's exact words were, "*it looks like War in Vietnam in there*.") He said that he was discovered by a Comcast cable worker who was scheduled to cut his cable on that day. Although Detective Carter could not get into details just yet, I had heard enough.

Before we could even view his body at March Funeral Home, Jamal had to buy a skull cap to cover the emptiness that used to be his skull.

This was February 1995 and just one tragedy in a series of tragedies in my life that would have me wondering if somebody had put a curse on my family. I've always had the feeling that my life was something out of a movie script. Full of drama and mayhem. My whole life as well as the lives of my brothers and sisters was always wracked with some sort of earth shattering event. No time for rest or planning in my life because just when you thought you had the game of life by the tail, something else happens that causes you to see things another way. As I hung up the phone with Detective Carter, as clear as day itself, I told myself that I gave up on my father before. This time I would not. **I would stop at nothing to find out who did this and why**.

Chapter Two

The year was 1972. Sweltering, hot ass July in
Baltimore, Maryland. I trace the beginning of my life
to all the stories that I have been told about my birth. I
was the third daughter of Leroy and Carolyn Lincoln.
As the story goes, my mother's pregnancy with me
was an easy one. I was born in a little over three
hours. My father, who worked as a taxi driver, wanted
my name to be Pamela after his first wife, but of
course, my mother wasn't having that. I weighed in at
five pounds and seventeen ounces at Lutheran Hospital
in West Baltimore. I was a happy child. One who
laughed easily and behaved well. I walked early,
talked early, developed early. In childhood photos, I
am playing cheerfully with my two sisters Marlene and
Poochie. Some photos show me smiling happily with
my mother or my father. My earliest child hood
memory is one that I can remember clearly.
We are living in a small row home on Lorraine
Avenue. It's a neighborhood diverse with both blacks
and whites who all share the same level of poverty. I
am in the basement with my two sisters. We are
supposed to be sleeping but we are being noisy as
usual, sneaking in and out of the bed, running back and

forth. I am all of three years old. Earth, Wind, and Fire are blazing at full volume on my parents stereo system upstairs and it is a sticky, sweltering, summer night. I hear my father's footsteps coming across the floor and my sisters and I scatter to our bed that the three of us share, in the basement. Instead of yelling for us to keep the noise down, he hollers out, "Who wants some beer?" All three of us start sprinting up the basement steps to get a sip of beer. In my three year old mind, I can not believe that although it's late, and we are not sleeping like we are supposed to be, my father rewards us with beer. As I'm running up the basement steps trying to keep up with my sisters, I trip over something and come crashing down on my face. Blood is everywhere and for the next couple of years, I have a smile that is missing the four teeth that were there before. After my mother tends to me with cold water and toilet tissue, I got my beer.

I remember my early childhood as one overflowing with music, parties that my parents gave, and the company of my two older sisters. Marvin Gaye, The Commodores, The Jacksons, Atlantic Starr is blaring on the eight-track stereo that is the pride and joy of my father. The house is packed with friends of my parents. The air is thick with the scent of Colt 45, whiskey, cigarettes, and weed. My sisters and I are supposed to be in bed but as usual, we are sneaking by the basement steps, peeping upstairs, taking in all the sights. My mother didn't work and whatever job my father did have was apparently not enough to keep up a family of five. We changed addresses at least four times before my sixth birthday. We lived in poverty where the rats invaded our home as if it were their own. One house we lived in was a row home on West Cold Spring Lane. What I remember most about this house were the huge rats that scattered about, day or night oblivious to the smell of humans. They simply were not even afraid of us. You couldn't just stomp your foot and scare them like you could with the mice. They were so rampant that these rats didn't hesitate in letting us know that this was their turf and we were invading it. My mother used to kill them by cornering them and hurling boiling water on them. The sound they made as they were being scalded to death was a cross between a baby crying and a cat hissing. To this day, I am terrified of rats. I get chills even passing by them in pet stores.

Two more sisters soon arrived before my fifth birthday. So now the house was filled with my parents and four children all under the age of eight. All girls, but we got along just fine. Family photos show the five of us together playing and smiling happily. With the exception of my older sister Marlene, none of us are in school and we amuse ourselves by playing together. It's 1977 and my family grows yet again with the birth of a brother, finally, and we all call him PJ. My father begins a new job driving a bus for Mass Transit Administration and things begin to look brighter for us financially. My parents soon decide to move their growing family to 3013 Presbury Street in West Baltimore. The end house boasts of having a huge yard, four nice sized bedrooms and a large eat in kitchen. It is here where my child hood really began to take shape. Although we are less than a mile from the major drug traffic on North Avenue, it is here where we call home for the next seven years. It is here where the hell starts and the nightmares of growing up in this family begin.

It's the first day of school. My mother attempted to allow us to enter kindergarten the previous year but after a few days decided that it was not for us. She wanted to prolong us going to school as long as possible. She was so used to us being around her that she was kind of nervous in allowing us to be around other kids. My older sisters had already started going to school and I was eager to follow in their footsteps. As my mother allowed me to put on my brand new school clothes that I got from Montgomery Wards, I excitedly anticipated walking to school with my sisters. I was especially close to my sister Poochie because we were not too far apart in ages. Although I was unusually shy and quiet, I couldn't help but be excited about finally going to school. I was determined to get excellent grades to make both my parents and my teachers proud. I attended Belmont Elementary School and lived a rather nerdy, quiet, existence. I was in first grade when I discovered that I loved to write. My teachers all commented that I had exceptional handwriting for my age. In fact, I used to wish that I would be caught doing some infraction where I would have to write out my punishment on the blackboard. While other kids thought this to be a cruel form of punishment, I secretly hoped that I would have the chance to show off my handwriting this way. I practiced writing my name in cursive, always professionally adding my middle initial to my work, even while in elementary school. I was always either drawing or writing on my notebook paper or book bag. I was the quiet child, the good child, and the child who never got into any trouble during my entire elementary school years. My favorite subject back then was math. I was always good with numbers and figuring things out in my head. I felt as though my brain was a sponge and I was ready to absorb anything. The type of child who loved to read more than anything else. Once I learned how to read, I realized that books could take me to places that I couldn't go, physically. I read everything I could get my hands on. I read the entire dictionary twice out of sheer boredom. I would confuse my brother and sisters with the new words that I had taught myself daily. You would rarely find me without a book in my hands. I had every *"Mother Goose"*, *"Little House on the Prairie",* or *Judy Blume* book I could find. I didn't ask for toys like other kids. I was satisfied with my Mother Goose book collection. Music was always playing somewhere in my house because of my father's love of music. I was forever singing along with the stereo. Once, my father even had me, along with my sisters, in a singing group for a group called, "The Future Now." Although the group went nowhere musically, it was quite an experience to hear a song on the radio where we sang background vocals. I remember I loved standing in front of that enormous microphone and singing my heart out while my father recorded us over and over to get the sound just right. I dreamed of being either a singer or a dancer. Just to be allowed to stay up late and perform in front of his friends was an honor to me. My father never made any real money from our brief stint in background singing, but the whole experience of being in front of a microphone is forever engraved in my memory.

Chapter Three

Around the age of six, my parents became committed
to a religion known nationally as Jehovah's Witnesses.
The Jehovah Witness faith teaches values that are
totally unlike any other religion that is practiced today.
We could no longer celebrate holidays, not even
birthdays. We had to go to meetings at the Kingdom
Hall on Sundays, Tuesdays, and Thursdays. We went
to Circuit and District conventions at least twice during
the year. My parents began dedicating their lives to its
teachings and they raised us to believe in them also. I
had no idea what I was being taught, never really
considered it at this young age. All I knew was that we
couldn't do things that the other kids in school were
doing. We did not pledge allegiance to the flag or take
part in any school functions, period. We could not
make friends with anyone else who did not practice
this faith either, so as a result, we were known in
Belmont Elementary School as the *"Jehovah Kids"*.
We were taught to be completely and totally different
from anyone of *"this world"*. I felt so alienated
because I was so different from my peers and
classmates. I wanted to be able to dress like they did,
talk like they did. I felt embarrassed to be seen

walking to the Kingdom Hall on a warm Thursday night while my classmates from the neighborhood could see us dressed in our Sunday Best. I felt embarrassed to be preaching from door to door handing out Watchtower and Awake magazines. I prayed that no one I knew from school would answer the door. Sometimes they did and I would hear about it all the next day at school. I was just a young child who realized right away that we were different from the other kids who went to school. We were not permitted to take part in any of the holiday functions, go on any field trips, or even participate in any after school programs at all. We were at school to learn and that's it. No fun or socializing because that was simply not tolerated. The Jehovah Witness faith teaches that any unnecessary involvement with people who are not of the same faith will sooner or later corrupt your beliefs. In school, when all the other kids were making Mother's Day Cards or exchanging Christmas Gifts, we either were separated from the class or stayed home altogether. No longer could we listen to *"debased"* music or watch anything on TV that had foul language, illicit sex, or violence. <u>*Anything*</u> that compromised our parents' religious beliefs had to go. I mean, we couldn't even watch "The Flintstones" because my parents didn't support the caveman theory of evolution. Even "The Smurfs" had to go because they believed that the illusion of magic was wrong. "A Charlie Brown Christmas" was banned from our house because it had the word "Christmas" in it. We were required to come straight home from school at all times. No excuses were tolerated since we had absolutely no reason to be late coming home from school. My parents believed that to *"spare the rod"* was spoiling the child. They didn't hesitate whatsoever in admonishing discipline whatever way they saw fit. One of the restrictions that hurt me the most was that we weren't allowed to even talk to our aunts, uncles, cousins, not even our grandparents. It didn't matter that most of them were Jehovah's Witnesses too, my mother just told us that they didn't like us anyway. We were the black sheep in the family. I would always think about my cousins and wonder if they were being brought up the same way we were. I fantasized about having an aunt or a grandmother that I could talk to. We were kept so tightly together that instead of us sticking together like my mother intended, we began to hate each other. My mother fed off of that hate and turned us against each other. It was so hard to talk to her or open your heart to her, not knowing if she would be telling my sisters or brothers everything that was said. There was so much *he say she say* in our family that it was nothing for us to go months without even speaking to each other.

Marlene began to fight back by coming home from school later than our three o'clock curfew. Now thirteen, she was attending Lemmel Junior High School and couldn't be easily monitored as we were. She would be late coming home for something as simple as walking home from school with someone and would be beaten. Since we only went to school and meetings at the Kingdom Hall, "punishments" mostly varied from going to bed early to doing the dishes for few weeks. But my parents number one discipline method was without a doubt, the belt. Even with the many beatings and punishments she got for coming home late, it could not dissuade her from wanting to get out and mix with people who were not Jehovah's Witnesses.

Teased just about all through school because she was an albino, Marlene began to take on a tough exterior to all those who didn't know her well. Her daily schedule consisted of coming home from school late, getting the mandatory beating from my mother or father, going to the meetings, getting another beating for going to sleep during the meeting, then going to bed. It was a daily occurrence. Once she even got a beating because she came home five minutes past her three o' clock curfew and that was only to get our parents an Anniversary gift. There were no excuses tolerated. The beatings just made her rebel even more. As a result, she began to run away from home. A lot. What I remember most about growing up with Marlene was all the beatings she got for *"not listening"* or *"not obeying the rules of the house."* Once she received seven beatings in one night, back to back, for things that happened years ago. After one such beating, she ran away from home yet again. Except this time charges were brought against my parents for child abuse. I remember her being put in a foster home and everything. I had to have been about seven or eight when my mother came back from one of Marlene's court hearings and told us that Marlene wouldn't be living with us any more. It devastated all of us. We cried along with my mother. Marlene was fourteen years old and could not take living there any longer. She could no longer take all the beatings and restrictions any more. After she left and was moved from foster home to foster home to group home to group home, we didn't keep in contact with her that much. Our contact with her was severely restricted because she was now thought of to be part of *"the world"* and not the Jehovah Witness faith. Marlene did come back home once at the age of 17 after she had given birth to her first son. Living on the streets and penniless, she hoped to convince my parents into letting her come back home for a while. My mother considered her a bad influence on us and my father literally had to pick her up, put her out on the porch with her newborn son in her arms and tell her never to come back. It was a horrible scene that I will never forget.

It was also during this time that my father began to spend less and less time at home. A heavy smoker of Kools cigarettes, my father found the craving virtually agonizing. He began secretly smoking again and hanging out with acquaintances from work. This was totally looked down on by the Jehovah Witness faith. Probably out of sheer embarrassment or maybe a desire for a change, he quit going to the meetings altogether. After the Elders in the congregation made frequent attempts to get in contact with him to discuss what was going on, he refused to meet with them. Ultimately, he was *"disfellowshipped"* from the religion. That means that no one can have any contact with you. No other Jehovah Witnesses were allowed to talk to him, be seen with him, or associate with him in any way shape or form. Most people who are disfellowsipped from the congregation usually sit way in the back when they do come to the meetings. When Marlene left, I began to get closer to my sister Poochie. We shared a room together, thought of ourselves as best friends instead of sisters. Back then, we were always together. In school, we both were especially bright. Both of us were in a program for gifted and talented kids called GATE. I even had an opportunity to get skipped up to Poochie's grade but my mother refused. Jehovah's Witnesses perceive education and school as unnecessary roadblocks to gaining a true relationship with Jehovah. Your relationship with Jehovah is far more valuable than getting good grades, college, even secular work. This was implanted into us from the time I can remember. As children, the only place we were allowed to play was either in the house or our front yard. It was the biggest yard that expanded from the front of the house all the way to the back of the house. Under no conditions were we allowed to go out of the fence. Even if we were playing ball and the ball accidentally went into the street, we had to ask our parents to retrieve it for us. All of us played together. Poochie, myself, Cocoa, Roshell, and PJ. Another brother, Kenneth, entered our family in 1979, bringing us to a family of seven.

In the yard we caught bees or dug for worms and insects in the dirt. We raced or caught lightening bugs at dusk. Because we were a large family, money was tight, and we didn't have the things that other people in the neighborhood had. One of the Witnesses in the hall gave us a bike to ride, but even with that, we had to ride it only on the sidewalk and only a few yards from our front porch. It was almost funny to see five kids sharing one bike that we rode from the porch to the pole in front of our yard. We weren't allowed to go any farther. Needless to say we didn't have much fun on that bike. I was totally okay with sitting in a corner, reading or daydreaming about something. Our lives were controlled like this: we went to school, came home, went to the Kingdom Hall, and out in Field Service on the weekends. During Summer Vacations we spent all of our time in the Field Ministry, averaging between sixty and ninety hours a month. Sometimes we went out in Field Service in the evenings after school. We would get up as early as five in the morning to do *"street work"*. That consisted of a lot of walking and standing in areas where a lot of people would be, reaching out to future bible studies. We would be standing downtown in front of Lexington Market or walking on the streets of North Avenue, seeking more bible study students. Although we were allowed to socialize with some of the other kids that were in the Hall, our friendships were limited to a select few that my mother thought were suitable for us. And whatever time that was spent with the other people in the Hall had to be supervised. I was in the fifth grade when I began to mature physically. Truly, the only thing that was growing were my breasts. I was so embarrassed because no one else in school was developing as fast as I was. My mother seemingly didn't notice because one of her friends from the Kingdom Hall had to buy my first bra. I remember her saying in front of me, *"Can't you see this child needs a bra?"* Even Poochie wasn't wearing a bra yet, so I really felt out of place. The first bra I got wasn't even a training bra like most girls usually start out with, but a B-cup bra. It was during this time that another family with kids finally moved across the street from us. Starving for some sort of contact other than each other, secretly, we slowly became friends. One of the kids, Richard, was a complete Michael Jackson fiend. This was 1983 when Michael Jackson's *"Thriller"* album completely ruled the airwaves. Everybody wanted to be like Mike. Of course, we weren't allowed to even listen to this album because of the song *"Thriller"*. When my mother saw the video and saw Michael dancing with people who were supposed to be dead, she completely banned that whole album from our house. Especially when she learned that Michael Jackson was supposed to be a Jehovah's Witness. Luckily, my father would sneak this album in anyway, and play it while she wasn't home.

My father was spending more and more time away from home and it was discovered that he had another girlfriend who had kids of her own. When my father left the Kingdom Hall, he also left us and moved in with his new girlfriend. My mother hated that he was gone and she held no punches in telling us that he was a *no good, so and so*. She told us that he chose to live with another family and didn't care at all about us. My mother was outraged and undeniably hurt because she had no job, no money, no food, nothing. He left us totally penniless. I remember the first thing to go was our telephone. My mother used to have to walk up the street to a pay phone just to make phone calls. Since he was *disfellowhipped,* our contact with him was limited anyway. Plus we all had the idea that he was an outsider to us. It was drilled into our heads that he was a no good father who rather spend his time and money on a family that he didn't even create. So of course, after hearing all of this constantly, we all grew to hate him. When he finally left, it was not too much of a loss because even when he was still living with us, he was always gone, working. Us kids just thought of it as a way to get away with more things that we normally couldn't. They would make up and break up so many times we lost count. Each time, my father would move back in, stay a few months, then move back out again. It was a cycle that we got familiar with whether we wanted to or not.

The first boy I ever liked was Richard. Looking back on it now, I liked the way he made me laugh and was easy to talk to. He didn't care that we were Jehovah's Witnesses and didn't tease us like everyone else did. He treated me like one of his guy friends instead of this petite female. I was so badly prepared around boys that it was laughable. I remember one day in school, he put his arm around me and I was terrified I was going to get pregnant! I had absolutely no awareness about boys, sex, puberty, nothing, even though my body was changing. Sex was definitely not something that was talked about in our house. Just the word *"sex"* was hardly ever even mentioned. What little information I did know came from the medical books I would read. I remember being completely shocked to read that a female bleeds once a month. I didn't even know what *ovulation* meant until I was out of High School. Sex was just something that you were not to discuss. If you had questions and asked about it, you were questioned for even bringing up the subject. Because of our excellent grades, Belmont Elementary gave Poochie and I the chance to attend one of the more prestigious schools in the area. They were even going to pay for our transportation and everything so there shouldn't have been any excuses in us not going.

Roland Park Middle School was at least two buses away and I remember thinking, *"we'll never make our three o'clock curfew. "* My mother agreed and decided to send us to the closest school in our neighborhood instead. Calverton Junior High School. By this time, Poochie was now attending Calverton and I wanted to follow her out like yesterday. I couldn't wait to be going to Junior High with her. Finally, after getting all A's on my report card in the sixth grade, I would be joining her at Calverton. I remember when I got that report card, I eagerly showed my parents. For some reason, my father was home that day. When I showed him that I received all A's, he ran outside to show his friends my report card. I recall him saying," Look at what *my girl* did!" I was so delighted and full of pride. Unfortunately, Richard would not be going to Calverton with us because his family would be moving away that summer. I cried the whole night when they packed up their belongings on the moving van. I thought Richard would be the only boy I ever liked. I thought no other boy would ever want me. Richard understood about us not being able to do normal kid stuff because of the sternness of our parents and our religion. I thought, there's no way nobody's going to ever want me because I can't stay out, I can't go to parties, I can't celebrate holidays, hell, I can't even stay after school for anything. Perhaps things will improve once I get to Junior High School with Poochie, I thought.

Chapter Four

I entered Calverton Junior High School at the top of my class in 701. I developed an even bigger interest in drawing. My art teacher Mrs. Brown noticed that I had extraordinary flair in drawing and suggested that I further my education in this field. Although I was flattered because I knew that I had a talent for drawing, I never even thought about what I would do with my life after high school. I already knew that Jehovah's Witnesses were not permitted to pursue any further education after twelfth grade, at least that's what I was told. So, I let the words of Mrs. Brown go in one ear and out of the other.

Meanwhile, Poochie who was now in the eighth grade, was not fitting in Junior High too well. She didn't mature physically as fast as I did and kids teased her ruthlessly. When people found out that we were sisters, they didn't think twice in letting us know who looked more mature. Poochie began to resent me for reasons I did not fully understand. To top this off, we were not the most fashionable kids in the class or the school for that matter. My mother was still on welfare, my father, although still working at MTA, was always broke. Either way, even if we could have afforded it, my parents would have never bought us the hottest clothes, so we had to get our school clothes from stores like *"Goldenbergs"* or *"K Mart."* Already used to being teased at elementary school, Poochie was the first to give in to people teasing her about the way she dressed. I was the next. I had this coat that had to have been at least one hundred assorted colors and even if it was ten degrees outside, when I got to the front of the school, I would take my coat off and freeze the rest of the way to avoid being teased by my peers. I had these boot tennis shoes that had the nerve to be white, and the sole on them were at least three inches thick. Honestly, I had to stomp my way to school. To keep up with what everybody else was wearing, sometimes I would stitch the *"Levi"* nametag over my *"Uncle Charlie's"* jeans that I wore. While everybody else wore Nike's and Adidas, we wore *"Fish Heads."* It's funny now, but I wanted to fit in so desperately. I wasn't sure of what was happening to me, but I knew that I was developing an interest in boys. I started to look at them in ways that I hadn't noticed before. Maybe it was all of the attention they were showing me, I don't know. I was scared of even kissing a boy, don't even mention sex. I had only scatterbrained ideas of what sex was supposed to be like in the first place. My mother told us that "being with a boy" hurts like hell. So that reminder was fixed in my brain for as long as I could remember. During one of Marlene's rare visits, Poochie and I had discovered that Marlene had been having sex because she was proudly sporting a bright red passion mark on her neck. Poochie decided that she wanted to experience what sex was like too, and she wasn't as nervous or petrified as I was.

One night after we came back from a six hour District Convention in Landover Maryland and everyone else had gone to sleep, Poochie told all of her dreams and wishes to me. She was sick of going to the Hall, sick of obeying all the rules and restrictions. She wanted to be allowed to talk on the phone with not only boys, but girls in her class as well. She was going crazy over the rule of not walking home from school with her new friend, Michelle. More importantly, we were tired of the beatings for every little mishap. Tired. Tired. Tired. Hell, Poochie figured if she was going to keep getting beatings, she may as well do things that were truly deserving of a full beating. I confessed that I was tired of living like this, too. She even said that maybe Marlene had done the right thing in leaving. Marlene was sporting new clothes, had her ears pierced and everything. And she appeared to be so much happier. It was driving us insane. That night, as we lay under the covers, we decided that we were going to defy our parents and the religion. I didn't know if I was going to go as far as really having sex with a guy, but I thought I was going to at least feel what a real kiss felt like. Poochie talked about this guy she thought was cute named John. John was in the ninth grade, kind of on the short side, but bowlegged in a sexy kind of way. Not too bad looking, but not a guy I thought was worth getting a beating for. I picked the worst *Bad Boy* I could find. A boy who was all of sixteen and in the ninth grade at Calverton. He lived on Baker Street, right around the corner from our house. He was enormous. Already a giant in junior high. With my four feet frame, I was a midget standing next to him. Tall, dark, fine-looking in a street, thuggish sort of way. Just the type of guy I was intrigued with at twelve. I noticed him studying me whenever he walked by our house to go to the store. Every girl in the neighborhood wanted him. God, he was fine! I didn't even like the girls across the street from us because they wanted him, too. Unlike us, they were allowed to stay outside well after dark. While Poochie chose John, I chose Gerald, who both just happened to be best boys. Together we embarked on a mission to find some excitement in our lives.

The next day, while we were walking home from school, we saw them further up the street and we caught up with them. Right away Gerald starts making remarks about what big titties I have. I kind of timidly laughed it off. I was so used to hearing plenty of *"mountain tittie"* jokes that his words only slightly annoy me. This was the kind of attention I was getting at twelve. Poochie puts it out there right away that we are ready to go with them over their house if no one's home. They start teasing us about being those *"Jehovah Girls"* who are too scared to try anything. They tell us that we are too young for them. Really, I *am* bluffing but I am more and more amazed at Poochie. I can tell she is not joking. She is really serious about going over his house. Wounded and pissed by the rejection, Poochie walks away mumbling that the next time she will not fail. She is determined to be taken seriously.

It's not until months later when we catch them off guard again. Schools were closed for a blizzard that blanketed the streets. My mother surprisingly allowed

us go out to play in the snow and not just in the yard, but we got to play throughout the streets of Grayson and Rosedale. So, while Poochie, myself, and our younger sister Cocoa play in the snow, who comes up the street but Gerald, John, and another friend of theirs from the neighborhood named Mike. I feel a snowball hit me on my ass. I turn and see Gerald smirking with his friends. I pummel him back with snowballs.
"So, you want to play, huh?" he grins.
I'm laughing mischievously. Out of nowhere, he grabs me and we both end up falling in the snow and I land lying right between his legs, on top of him. He doesn't make an immediate attempt to get off of the ground and I can feel without a doubt, a brick rising between his legs. I am silently mortified thinking, *if my mother could see me now, lying out in the street between Gerald's legs.* When he finally let me get up, he began to pound me with snowballs and slams me to the ground between his legs yet again. When I get the chance to see what Poochie is doing, I see that John and Mike are doing her the same way. Shocked but intrigued at the same time, I let Gerald sneak a few feels of my breast, pretending not to notice what he is doing. After about an hour, we know we better head home before my mother begins to look for us considering it is dark outside and my mother did let us play outside without having to stay in the yard.
That night Poochie and I talk about what had happened. Excitedly, we discussed how hard their dicks felt against their snowsuits. (God, remember in the eighties when teenagers sported full snowsuits like two year olds? Those were the days!) We were giddy and nervous at what all of this would lead to. We had

shown them that we were not the scared little girls that they thought we were by allowing them to do this. It was a fantastic feeling. One that Poochie desired more and more of.

A few weeks later, the plan was set. We told our mother that we were going to the library on North Avenue to do some research for a school project. Instead we hooked up over John's house while his parents were gone. We brought Michelle there for Michael to entertain. Right away, Gerald takes me into John's basement bathroom. While everyone else is running around, catching feels of asses and titties, me and Gerald are chilling in the bathroom. Gerald is cool and gentle as he puts his arm around me. I'm shaking like a leaf because I've never in my life been this close to a boy before, and it's not like he's twelve like me, he's sixteen, and I'm terrified because he is doing his best to get my jeans down. I move his hand away, he moves it back, I move his hand away, he moves it back. Finally, he says, "Since you're not gonna let me put it in, let me suck on these." I'm like, *what?!* Other than mothers who breastfeed, I didn't even know that this was something that was done, a part of sexual play. He lifts up my shirt, unhook my bra with ease and my bare breasts are out in the open like a motherfucker. It's pitch black but I still feel naked and exposed as hell. He starts sucking my nipples and trust me, pain was *definitely not* what I felt. After he does this for a good while, his hand goes traveling down to my zipper again. I still move his hand away, but after a few more tries at this I finally agree to let him take my jeans down but he is only to touch me there and *absolutely not* put his *"thing"* in me. He agrees, and I allow him to pull my jeans and my panties down, all the way to my freaking ankles. "You damn sure don't feel like no twelve year old." he pants. He is lying on top of me on the cold bathroom floor and there is positively no mistake in what I feel growing from him. I'm asking myself, *when did he take his pants down?* I'm wondering this when he says, "Let me turn the light on. I want to see what you look like." Shy as hell, I beg him not to and we debate this for a while. Finally, he convinces me that he'll only leave the light on for a sec. When flicks on the light switch, I automatically look down at his penis and for the first time in my life, I see what a real penis looks like when completely aroused. Right then, I totally change my mind about anything that I agreed to do. I make up my mind that I am certainly not going to let him stick that huge thing in me! I quickly start making excuses about how I have to go home. It's getting late, I'm too scared, I changed my mind, I'm too cold, I tell him anything to get out of that bathroom. While he is convincing me to do otherwise, all of a sudden, the door flies open and I see John and Michael laughing their asses off! I am laying there, shirt up, pants and panties down to my ankles, and Gerald starts trying his best to cover us up with a short towel. I prayed that I could just sink into the floor. I'm so humiliated and embarrassed as I see the stunned look on Michelle's and Poochie's faces. Their jaws are to the floor. I am the youngest one there and I am managing to go further than any of them. After Gerald begs them to close the door back, I'm in no mood to continue this discovery of bodies, so Gerald reluctantly lets me back up to pull my clothes up. When we finally leave out of

John's house, both Poochie and Michelle asks me how was it to have had sex.

"But, I didn't do nothin. His thing looked too big. There was no way I was gonna let that thing inside of me!" I protest.

They laugh but stare at me approvingly because I still had managed to go further than any of them had been. They start allowing me to hang with them in their little clique and I was so impressed. When we came home that day, late as hell, although my mother didn't really suspect anything, she said we could no longer leave out for that long without taking my sister Cocoa with us. That was major damage because Cocoa was known for being the snitch in the family. So we were not able to get away to see them for quite some time and when we finally did, it would be the last, in more ways than one.

Chapter Five

The whipping went on forever, it seemed. My mother angrily swings the belt on both of us and we scream out in pain. We had been caught walking home from school with Michelle and this was the dreaded punishment that we received. Poochie was so pissed after the beating that she decided to run away from home. She was sick and tired of all the rules that she thought were totally ridiculous. I tried to talk her out of it, but her mind was made up. I didn't want to be without her since we shared so many secrets. So reluctantly, I decided to go with her even though I was scared to death and we had no plans whatsoever. We just craved to get out of the prison that we felt we were in. While my mother was off in the basement somewhere, we jetted out the back door with just the clothes on our backs and headed around the corner to Michelle's house. Michelle knew all about how it was living over our house and she felt sorry for us totally, and even explained to her mother about what had been going on. We tearfully told Michelle and her mother that we had just gotten a beating for walking home from school with Michelle, someone who was not one of Jehovah's Witnesses. Michelle's mom couldn't understand why we were being forbidden from hanging around her daughter. I mean, Michelle was an honor roll student, with no problems, who just wanted to be friends with us. Disturbed, her mom called my mother over to discuss this reasonably. When my mother arrived, we could see from the look on her face that as soon as we were back home, we were going to be in even more trouble. We cried for Michelle's mom to not make us go back home because we knew what would happen as soon as we got in the door. My mother would promise nothing to no one. Not to Michelle's mother and certainly not to us. She basically told her mother where to go and to mind her own business. After hours of us crying and airing out our frustrations, we realized that we really couldn't just stay over Michelle's house. We had no choice but to go back home. As soon as we got back, my mother had the extension cord laid out on the bed. She beat us with all of the anger she could muster. This was not the first time an extension cord had been used and it would surely not be the last.

I began the eight grade with an aggressive attitude. For the first time, although I was placed in 801, the class for Calverton's brightest students, my grades began to fall. After scoring almost all A's in the seventh grade, my grades dropped dramatically. I went from A's to C's and D's. I no longer cared about school or pleasing my teachers or parents. I felt, what's the point in getting good grades? I'm not going to college or nothing anyway.

I finally met a friend who I could relate to who seemed to be going though as much problems at home as I was. Her name was Shanice Merry. Her mother was a junkie who basically didn't care much what her daughter did. Shanice had already had sex with a number of guys, smoked weed, didn't have a curfew, and her main goal in life was to have a baby. I made her my best friend and we began to share everything. I had to explain to her why I wasn't able to hang out, or give out my telephone number. She understood all of this and sympathized with me. One day I even hooked school with her for the first time. Naturally, I was caught almost immediately. My father actually came home for the honor of beating me for that one. Poochie and I were so sick of getting punished all the time for every little mishap. We were just so tired and miserable from not being able to talk to anybody, go outside, or have any friends that we didn't have to hide from my mother. The isolation was driving us crazy to the point where we didn't even care anymore about the consequences of doing what we wanted to do.

"Poochie and I are waiting on the back porch. Waiting for Mama to hear this new music that we are dying to listen to. Poochie has recorded this song over and over and each time I hear it, it puts me in a better mood. It makes me forget that I'm different from everyone else in the neighborhood. The beat is undeniable. As my mother comes to the screen door, Poochie pushes play on the portable recorder. "Hard Times" by Run DMC plays through the recorder. Like I said, the beat was undeniable. Poochie and I are bouncing to the beat, snapping our fingers, mouthing the words, every lyric.
"Shut it off!" my mother says.
"I don't like it," she sighs.

Just like that, we aren't allowed to listen to rap music. But me being the music fanatic that I am, I sneak and listen to L.L. Kool J's "I Need Love" under my pillow with headphones."

Almost a year had passed since Gerald and I had the incident in the bathroom over John's house. Now after seeing him in the hallway at school, he asked me if I was still a *"little girl."* "Are you gonna let me pop your cherry or what?" he whispers while cornering me against the lockers. I was now thirteen, but looked sixteen. Daring, brave, and pissed off at the world. He was seventeen and probably still in the ninth grade. He told Poochie and I to meet him over his house after school. We both knew that this would mean that we would break our curfew if we stopped over his house and that would certainly mean another beating. But for some reason, we didn't even let that scare us. We didn't even think about what would happen. We just didn't care.

It was September 19, 1985. Gerald had brought one of his boys home with him named Antoine who was supposed to be for Poochie. After school, we followed him home and found ourselves in his house, alone. His parents were nowhere in sight. Gerald and I immediately went upstairs to his parents' room, on his parent's bed. We sort of picked up where we left off last fall, but I chickened out again when I felt him trying to push himself in me. For some reason, I thought I would bleed on his parents' bed and it would possibly get on my clothes and my parents would know for sure what I had done. I was terrified again and went into defensive mode. I guess you could say I was the biggest tease he ever met because he was used to getting any girl he wanted. Frustrated, he just gave up.

As he was lying there sulking, we heard a car pull up. He looked out the window and discovered his mother was home early. He rushed us all outside yelling for us to run and we all snuck out the back door. I didn't even have a chance to wash the sweat off my face or anything. We were more than two hours late from school. Complete and total disobedience. As we walked home, Poochie decided that we were going to need a first class story to get us out of a beating this time for sure. She mentioned that since I looked all sweaty, we were going to say that a boy had tried to rape me. It sounds completely off the wall and bizarre for us to have come up with a lie so bold and bald-faced, but at the time, we would have done whatever it took, not to get another beating with the dreaded extension cord. After we came home and told our parents this fantastic story of Gerald choking me, hitting me, stealing my necklace, and trying to rape me, my father did the last thing we expected. He said something that was worse than what a beating could ever be. My father decided to go back over there and meet face to face, the boy who did this to his daughter. I swallowed the enormous knot in my throat as Poochie and I pointed out to him where Gerald lived. As my father threw accusations all in his face, Gerald wisely stayed behind his screen door and insisted that he didn't rape or hit anybody. I couldn't even look him in his face. My father threatened to yank off the screen door and go up side his head with it. Gerald shut the door in his face. Once we arrived home, it only got worse. It was the only time I ever saw tears in my father's eyes.

"Carolyn, call the police."

Everything just happened so fast. We found ourselves at the police station filling out reports of the rape that never happened. They took pictures of me and everything. I just had this complete, numb feeling while Poochie was ecstatic that we had managed to get out of a beating. Gerald was arrested and stayed locked up until his parents bailed him out of jail. He was forced to not have any contact with us or come within a certain amount of feet from us which I'm sure he had no problem with. To make matters worse, my parents explained to the school principal what had happened and informed them that Gerald was not to even look my way. All of this was done in front of Gerald who assured everybody that he would comply with whatever. It was a complete mess.

Only after the trial when Gerald *was* found guilty did we finally admit to my mother what we had done. She told us that we didn't have to inform the court of anything. Hell, she didn't like him anyway. She insisted that we hadn't done a thing wrong because he was headed for jail anyway, she reasoned. I never thought that we would really get away with lying on somebody and they would actually go to jail for it, but Gerald was sentenced to eighteen months in Waxter Center for Boys.

I felt so guilt-ridden about what I had done that I couldn't eat or sleep for days. My mother told me to snap out of it before my father suspected that something was wrong. We had managed to lie to our parents, the lawyers, and a judge who all believed our story. I couldn't believe that I had done this to a boy who I had in fact, begun to like. He remained my ultimate crush for years and years and I was so distraught by the harm that we had done to him that I couldn't put him out of my mind. I refused to even look at any other boys and convinced myself that I would save myself for him to show him that I was so sorry for what I had done. I gave up on the boyfriend game that Poochie was playing. However, Poochie was just beginning. She told me that while I was with Gerald, she had been trying to get her groove on with Antoine in the other room. No matter what she did to have him pay attention to her, he refused. She complained that he eyed the TV instead of her, the entire time. I couldn't see why boys weren't interested in her, neither could she. It wasn't like she was ugly or anything. Feeling rejected and ugly and now more determined than ever, she just had to find a boy that would like her, she thought.

Chapter Six

We called him *"Dusty David"*. Dusty because he wore the same black and white Easter sweat suit damn near everyday. He was the type of guy that no girl in the neighborhood wanted to fuck with. He reeked of urine and body odor in the fifth degree. Only fourteen, he wasn't the cutest nigga in the world. He didn't go to school, and just drifted in the neighborhood. He lived with his foster parents around the corner from us on Bloomingdale Road. Yet, Poochie decided he was going to be her next target. She chose somebody who she knew was not going to reject her. After she secretly started sneaking to see him, I would cover for her at first. But after a few times of her sneaking off, I got tired of lying for her. I was scared I was going to get in trouble for her because she was taking even bigger risks to sneak off and go see him. She would say she was going across the street to the store and be gone for an hour or she would sneak out when my parents weren't home. On one occasion, in the summer as usual, when she came back from seeing him, she told me that she was no longer a virgin.
Totally naive and unbelieving her, I asked," How do you know for sure?"

She said, "Trust me, I'm sure. He slammed me on it over and over to make sure."
I was totally shocked but envious at the same time because she had definitely went further than I had. She told me that oh yeah, it really does hurt the first time. I was so stunned at her incredible attitude about the whole thing. But there was one major problem. Dusty David had left this huge passion mark on her neck that was almost impossible to hide. Poochie panicked, as my parents would surely see it. Frantically, we tried to hide it with makeup, toothpaste, anything. Unsurprisingly, my mother found out first. She totally lost it after Poochie admitted to having sex with David. Too angry to even go up side Poochie's head, my mother screamed every foul name she could think of at her. ***"SLUT! WHORE! TRAMP!"***, she screamed. Poochie just hung her head, too shamed for words. My mother promptly informed both of us that my father would be handling this once he came home form work. That literally scared the shit out of us. I knew I would get in trouble also because I hadn't told them what she had been doing.
Sobbing on the front porch, Poochie actually begged my mother, on her knees, not to tell my father what she had done. My mother promised she wouldn't tell because even she knew that my father would treat her totally different and possibly snap her neck like a twig if he knew his fourteen year old daughter was having sex. We didn't know that my mother did not keep this secret until later that day after we got back from the Kingdom Hall. All we heard was my father yell for us to get our asses out of bed and get downstairs. The look on my father's face told us that he knew

everything. At first, he tried his best to remain calm talking to her, but when Poochie made the mistake of saying that she thought David had loved her, my father just lost it. He told us to get the hell out of his sight. Poochie was too slow in moving and my father kicked the door on her head, leaving a nasty lump. Then he lost it.

Despite the beating she received that night from one of those orange heavy-duty extension cords, she would not stop sneaking out to see David. From then on she seemed determined to get a reputation for being the easiest lay in the world. She would run away from home often and stay out all hours of the night. Sometimes she stayed with teachers from school. Sometimes she slept on the streets to avoid coming home. I would miss her so much. I just couldn't understand what she wanted out of the streets. I couldn't understand why she just *had* to have a boyfriend, all the time.

Of course, all of this had to be confessed to the Elders in the congregation for us to be "formally" disciplined. After an especially intense Committee Meeting with the Elders in the congregation where she had to explain in detail not only how she had had sex, but why, how did it feel, etc, she was *disassociated* from the Kingdom Hall. My mother told us that since Poochie was disassociated, we could no longer associate with her outside of the house. If I were to see her in school, or outside some where I was not allowed to even speak to her. None of my brothers and sisters were. She was to be known as the *"slut"* in the family. Totally ostracized by us. This only estranged her even more. We started to lose the closeness that we once shared and she became more quiet and isolated from everyone. She would have sex with just about anybody who asked. Men, boys from school, or boys from the neighborhood, even boys from the Kingdom Hall, which was completely shocking for me because I thought they were so holy and righteous. By the time Poochie was fifteen, she had had sex with over ten boys already and had venereal disease after venereal disease. It was nothing for my mother to have to take her back to the doctor for venereal cramps she was always having. After each and every doctor visit for gonorrhea, she would receive the now expected beating. My father eventually just gave up and moved back in with another girlfriend, leaving my mother to raise us herself. However, he would make the occasional visit to throw the belt around when he felt it was necessary.

After Poochie was caught having sex with some boy in the house, my mother administered a beating on her that was so bad, I gave up counting the hits after one hundred. I listened and Poochie wasn't even crying no more, just whimpering and gasping. When my mother finally stopped, she had to sit down and rest from exhaustion. She left Poochie alone and went upstairs. After about thirty minutes, when I opened the door, all I saw was an open window. Poochie had run away yet again, but this time the whole routine of calling the police and filling out a missing person report would be somewhat changed. This time Poochie did exactly what Marlene did to get away. She had done what we had promised our mother we would *never* do. She told Michelle's mom what had happened and showed her the bruises, the welts, the cuts. Some of them were old, some of them were new. Her mom called the police and a warrant was issued. When the cops came to our door the next day looking for my mother, everyone was shocked because nobody expected Poochie to do this. We all had witnessed how hurt my mother was when Marlene had done the exact same thing years earlier. Bewildered, my mother turned herself in to face charges of child abuse.

My father was home that day and he was so upset, he ordered myself and my younger sister Cocoa to go looking for Poochie. He told us if we found her to give her an ass kicking that she would never forget. Somehow, we located her walking with some friends of hers and we proceeded to give her the ass kicking that my father ordered. Her friends jumped in and it was an all out brawl on the streets of Rosedale Avenue. And just like that, Poochie became the enemy. It was sister against sister. Cocoa and I ignored her tears of surprise. I'll never forget the look on her face as she realized that things would never be the same between us again. This time she was gone for good.

Chapter Seven

When Poochie was taken out of the home and placed with another foster family, it totally crushed me. Although I was angry for her pressing charges against my mother, I missed her tremendously. I saw it as an insult to our friendship. A slap in the face. Just like Marlene, Poochie was hated by our family. We would see her walking on the street and we would look the other way. We treated her like total shit, we even started rumors about her throughout the neighborhood. All the while, my mother encouraged this on. She was royally pissed because now she had two child abuse charges on her record. Although I still secretly missed Poochie, I could see that she was affected by what we were doing to her. To this day, I don't think she fully recovered from it. She was never the same. She would come around to visit every so often when she was allowed to. I was so jealous of the new clothes and shoes and money she was receiving from her foster parents. I was so envious because she actually had a ten o'clock curfew and was allowed to have a steady boyfriend and everything. She would happily brag to us how she was now going to Carver High School and studying Cosmetology. But despite all of the fun and bliss she appeared to be having, Poochie still missed us terribly and wanted to come home. My mother told us that Poochie was not a welcome member in this family and we were to treat her as such. We were not permitted to talk to her or say anything to her. Once she even visited us on her own and although she was allowed in the house, it became clear that my mother wasn't going to say one word to her. Poochie left in tears. I wanted to at least tell her that I didn't feel that we should be treating her this way, but I didn't say a word.

When it was discovered that she was pregnant at sixteen, my mother felt that Poochie was *"bad association"* for us. She was totally banished from the house and I was not allowed to have any contact with her. A former Honor Roll student, Poochie ultimately dropped out of school in the eleventh grade and moved in with my older sister Marlene, who was now living in the Lexington Terrace Housing Projects.

Marlene hadn't fared too well in life since leaving home at the age of fourteen. Marlene now had already dropped out of high school shy of only two months from graduation, given birth to one son at the age of seventeen; the father was nowhere in sight. In fact, my oldest nephew has never even laid eyes on his natural father. Marlene was now on welfare and pregnant with her second son. Her new beau had taken a liking to her and took her under his wing. He would show her the *real* ways of the world.

Life pressures had begun taking its toll on her and she, along with her boyfriend had begun using heroin, to lessen the pain of looking in the mirror and facing life everyday. She remained a well-known fixture on the second floor Lexington Street Building for a number of years. This is where she chose to bring up her boys where drugs were out of control in the West Side high rises of Baltimore City. She took pity on Poochie and decided to let her live with her instead of just living from one foster home or group home. Poochie willingly agreed to stay.

Somehow I managed to make it through the eighth grade at Calverton without Poochie. Poochie had screwed nearly every guy in the neighborhood and a number of boys at Calverton. My mother decided that it was time to pull me out of the school and away from Shanice as well, so instead of finishing the ninth grade at Calverton, I was given the option of attending high school early at Walbrook High. I accepted, just to get away from everything. I only attended Walbrook for a few months when my parents decided that it was time to get out of the city altogether.

My father had recently moved back in and began making changes in everybody's life. Somehow he persuaded my mother to move out into suburbia Owings Mills in a three bedroom apartment. All of a sudden, my brothers and sisters realized that they were serious this time and we would be leaving 3013 Presbury Street. I was filled with feelings of sadness, and anxiety but I was open to whatever the future would hold. From what my parents kept saying, we would be in a very pleasant neighborhood with trees and tranquility. I had no choice but to look forward to it. It's not like I had lots and lots of friends who were going to miss me. We were still going to the Hall faithfully and my mother decided that she was going to travel back and forth to this congregation, by bus, if she had to because all of her friends and acquaintances were here. So at least we would still visit the city from time to time, I thought. Maybe it was time for a change.

Chapter Eight

No one told us that this new fancy home we were moving into was the tiniest three bedroom apartment on the face of this earth. I don't know what my parents were thinking when they decided to put three teenage girls in one little room. Our beds were so close by one another it was almost like we were in a prison dorm room. My two brothers shared a room that was even smaller than ours. All of us were used to living in a four bedroom row home, but now it *really* seemed like prison. In the apartment's defense, the neighborhood was nice and peaceful and we were close to stores that you never see in the city. Yet we had no car and just my father's salary to take care of us. Somehow we all tried to fit into this neighborhood where we knew we did not belong and could not afford. More expensive than the rowhome we were formerly living in, my parents bickered frequently about money. Barely making ends meet, my father would pay the rent when he felt like it. Even if that meant him paying it on the last day of the month as opposed to the first of the month, when it was due. Having good credit meant nothing to them. Us kids had so many bills that were fraudulently in our name that we didn't even realize that our own credit would be screwed up before we were even old enough to apply for a credit card. Soon we were getting monthly eviction notices. I was attending a high school where I felt totally out of place with all the middle class black kids. I stayed completely to myself and tried to keep a low profile, not even attempting the slightest gesture of friendship with anyone. I was failing almost every subject not only because I had an *I-don't-need-an-education-because-I'm-not-going-to-college-anyway-attitude*, but also because the county schools in Owings Mills gave a more thorough education than Baltimore City Public Schools. Suddenly, I was faced with trigonometry and biology that I had never had at Walbrook. I mostly just drifted through the ninth grade and began the tenth grade with the same *"whatever"* attitude.

The only subject I got A's in was art. I was in the tenth grade when I finished an art project four months before it's due date. We had to sketch a portrait using nothing but pencil for the detail. It was a three month assignment and in two weeks, I had composed a portrait of Janet Jackson, Whitney Houston, and Anita Baker. I worked on it in my room every day just for relaxation since I didn't go outside much. Everybody in my family told me how excellent it looked and that I had some serious talent. I knew that I could draw because my room was covered not with celebrity posters (which we were definitely not allowed to have on the wall anyway) but all my sketches that I drew. From cartoon characters to still life pictures enhanced with colored chalk. My mother had even framed some of them. It was just something I did to relax. When I turned in my assignment and showed Mr. Jensen that I was working on another one, he was astonished. Impressed, he stopped what he was doing and marched me to the guidance counselor's office. He talked to me about this art school in Atlanta Georgia. If I was interested he could pretty much get me into a full paid scholarship program right after high school, he mentioned. I never even thought about it because I knew my mother would never let me attend. I remember when I showed her the papers, all she said was, "Atlanta, Georgia is so far away." When Mr. Jenson asked me what had I decided, I told him the truth. I told him that I couldn't go to college because I was one of Jehovah's Witnesses and I couldn't pursue any further education after the mandatory twelve years of school. He gave me this peculiar gaze and told me to think on it some more. I never even thought twice about it because I knew I would never be allowed to go.

Amazingly, during the summer I was allowed to work for the first time. I worked as an aide at Rosewood Center, a facility that took care of people with mental and physical handicaps. I didn't care where I would be working, as long as I had my own money finally to do whatever I wanted with. Amongst my brothers and sisters, I was the first to actually have a job. My mother had no choice to agree when the school offered it as part of its summer program. Besides, we were starving to death and of course, I would have to pay my share of rent, food, and utilities. I paid my mother fifty dollars out of my two hundred fifty every two weeks. I finally was able to buy the clothes, shoes, and things I wanted so I could finally stop looking like the bum that I did. I did not miss one day of work and I worked all summer long.

Within a few months, my father had moved out yet again leaving my mother to raise us alone. We were so used to the routine of him moving in and moving out that it didn't bother us much. This time she had no job, no car, nothing. So she headed back to the place where she knew she would get help. The local welfare office. Still, the monthly check that she got from them was not enough to make ends meet. Eating cornbread and plain white rice for the second night in a row in a hot ass apartment where the gas and electric had been shut off, my mother had this look of total hopelessness on her face. I guess moving to the county was not such a swell idea after all. My father came and went as he pleased. They fought all the time. We were poor, starving, miserable and crammed up into this tiny ass apartment like sardines. The silence alone was suffocating us. Somehow we still managed to catch the subway and two buses to get to each meeting three times a week. My mother was determined to continue going to this congregation even though there was at least two other congregations much closer to our home. If not for going to school or to the Kingdom Hall three days a week, we were bored to death. When my mother found out that our lease was not going to be renewed because of a pattern of paying the rent late, she knew she had to do something. She found work as a house cleaner and a babysitter and was receiving a welfare check as well. My father was finally forced to pay child support, taken directly from his check, which he was not too pleased about. She even found another home further out in the suburbs of Reisterstown where the landlady was not too picky about credit checks. She saved up some money and was able to buy her first car ever. The next thing I knew we were moving again, this time without my father. It was the first place that she had gotten entirely on her own, in her own name, without my father around. She was proud of herself and vowed to make changes to her life and our lives as well. The first thing she cut out was this extra long commute from Owings Mills to Baltimore to go to the Kingdom Hall. We started attending a congregation that was closer to our home. They helped us move into our new home and get settled.

So by all accounts we were doing much better financially than we ever had with my father being around. It was no secret that he now had a serious drug problem and had many girlfriends that he didn't hesitate to flaunt in my mother's face. All of us as kids would listen to the endless bickering from my mother about him and we grew to detest him like she did. It was a common saying that *"your father ain't nothing but a junkie and always will be."* We believed her when she told us relentlessly that he didn't care about us. We hardly ever saw him and when we did, we let it be known that he was not welcome back into our lives. We still respected him, out of fear, but we treated him like he was not even there when he did come to visit.

Chapter Nine

On one rare occasion when my mother could see that I
was especially miserable and depressed, she allowed
me to catch the bus to go visit Poochie and her new
son. My mother wanted to use her as an example as to
why I should get myself together and focus on what
she wanted me to do after graduation which was to
become a full time regular pioneer in the ministry. At
the time, I thought that was what I was supposed to do
with my life so I didn't even imagine doing anything.
Poochie was expected to give me a lecture on how it's
not easy to raise a kid all alone, on welfare. But when
I visited her, she was happier than I had seen her in a
while. She was cuddled up with her boyfriend and
their newborn son, Anthony, looking peaceful, like she
was on cloud nine. We caught up on old times and she
said she was happy that she had finally left home and
she had what she had always wanted all along. She
said she could never return to that prison. Besides, she
was fine where she was.
Looking at her situation, I could see her point. I was
still stuck on Gerald, a boy I hadn't even seen in over
two years. I still felt bored and unhappy with my life
and I vowed to fix it. I wanted to be like her, not with

a baby living in the projects, but I wanted her freedom. I would have done anything to for once, be one of those kids that stood out on the corner having nothing to do. I wanted to be like her or at least get as close as we once were. I told her that I would sneak back over there if I had to. I couldn't understand why I had to beg and plead just to see my own sister. After visiting her in the projects, despite the filth of the conditions she was living in, I realized that she had more freedom than I ever had. I was tired of playing games with all this strictness and niceness. I was going to do what I wanted regardless of the consequences. *I couldn't take it anymore.*

I entered Franklin High School in the eleventh grade with a chip on my shoulder. I finally had the hottest gear that all the rich kids were wearing. I had the *leather bomber jackets, the red, knee high, city rider boots, all the latest tennis shoes.* I still expressed my *"whatever"* attitude, except this time I disrespected teachers, too. My younger sister, now in the ninth grade, attended with me and we began to *"rule the school".* For the first time in my school years, I wasn't the quiet kid in the back of the room. Cocoa and I began to cut class, hook school, get into fights, and become all out rebels. The only thing we had no control over was that we still had to go the dreaded Kingdom Hall meetings. We hated the whole routine. We would dread the days that we had to go to the Kingdom Hall. We preferred our daily routine of coming home from school, putting our books on the table, and watching music videos. **We would dance our asses off!** Myself, Cocoa, and Roshell dancing our way to perfection. I would dream of being a singer

or a choreographer. I mean, MC Hammer or
Oaktown's 357 had nothing on us! We were female
Bobby Browns, I swear! We used to get down, having
fun. I just wanted to rebel in any way I knew how.
The first event I felt like I had to complete was finally
losing my virginity. I responded to the first guy who
showed an interest in me. His name was Donnell and
he was not in anybody's class because he was too old
to go to school. He was twenty and I was fifteen. He
lived just a few houses up from mine and within a
matter of days I was sneaking talking to him on the
phone. Nothing particularly attracted me to him other
than his height. He stood well over six feet tall. I was
so young, so green, I didn't even care that much about
myself to realize that he only wanted one thing from
me. Right off the bat he let it be known that he wanted
to have sex with me. I was so curious about sex and
boys in general so it didn't take much persuasion for
him to get me into bed.
I don't know what I was thinking when I thought I
could sneak a twenty year old man into my mother's
house while she was at work. I hooked school and
made plans to meet him over my house. It was the
summertime, as usual, and I answered the door in these
short, short, Daisy Dukes. Right away, he lifted me up
on his shoulder and carried me upstairs to my
bedroom.
It took forever to convince him that I was indeed a
virgin. Even then, he hesitated, but only for a moment.
He wasn't too enthused either after he discovered how
old I was. He said he would take it slow and proceeded
to put his lips on me, *everywhere*. And I do mean
everywhere. He said he wouldn't fuck me, just yet,

because I wasn't ready for it. He said he wanted me to think about this day some more and he would come back tomorrow. Then I would be ready. After a few hours of touching, feeling, rubbing, kissing, but no sex, I was in infatuated puppy love. I even called Poochie and told her what I was doing, let her speak to him and everything. She wasn't too thrilled about me being in the house with a man five years my senior. After he left, I was just about to change my clothes and meet him back over his house, when my mother came in the door. In her hand she was carrying the largest, ugliest, auto wrench I had ever seen. Never really a good liar, my bowels turned to water.

"Where is he?!"

"Where is who?"

"Tia don't play dumb with me. I'm not in the mood for jokes. Where is he?!"

"Nobody was here, Mama!"

Out of nowhere, my sister Cocoa comes out of the basement. I went into shock as I realized that she had been in the house, where we were, the whole time. I should have known that my mother was smarter than me. I should have known that Cocoa had been eavesdropping on our conversations since the first phone call. I should have known that Mama would send her to spy on me. But there was nothing I could say. Plus my mother told me that Poochie had called her at work and snitched that I was in the house with a twenty year old man. My mother told me to get out of her house, don't come back. I walked to the closest shopping center to beg for bus fare to get to Marlene's house. Marlene welcomed me with open arms and at first, I was happy to be out of that house. When I told

Donnell what had happened, he said it was over between us because he could go to jail over something like this. Completely heartbroken, I stayed with Marlene for about a week. Eventually, my mother came and picked me up to bring me back home, but the damage was done. If our relationship was simmering before, it was done now. My younger sister Cocoa idolized me to no end and I noticed that she copied everything I did. So it was only a matter of time before she was sneaking off to be with some boy somewhere.

Despite the regular beatings that we still received, we still persisted in doing our own thang. It drove my mother crazy and now we became known as the "*sluts and whores*" in the family. I hated when my mother called me these names, considering I wasn't even having sex yet. My mother never let me forget that I was to be the one to set the right example in the family and I was screwing up big time. I didn't want to set an example for anyone. I just wanted to have some freaking freedom. I mean, I had to quit two jobs because I wasn't allowed to work on Kingdom Hall nights. And besides, I had to be in at eight o'clock anyway. We still were not allowed to have friends so it was extra brutal during the summer. I felt like I was going to die from the isolation. I was on a mission to get out of that house one way or another.

Chapter Ten

I barely made it out of the eleventh grade at Franklin.
My grades sucked big time, I had just managed to slide
into the twelfth grade. I didn't have any real plans
after high school. Really, I just planned to get a
regular job doing I had no idea what, and get my own
place out Towson. I had no real job skills and no plans
to further my education any longer than was necessary.
Just one more year to go, was all that stayed on my
mind during the summer of 1989. Amazingly, my
mother allowed me to visit Poochie in the city more
and more often and when I did, she introduced me to a
friend of her new boyfriend. Poochie now had a
daughter in addition to her son that she was raising.
She lived on welfare with her boyfriend's mother, his
two sisters, and his cousin in the Saratoga Street
Housing Projects. Despite her situation, I looked up to
her and envied the freedom she had to come and go as
she pleased. I declared as much to her and she
introduced me to her boyfriend's cousin who was also
staying there.
Antione was just a year older than I was, but we had
absolutely nothing in common. I would literally sneak
to get on the phone with him and he would say maybe

two words to me. Maybe he was as shy as I was but we had totally no chemistry. I got bored with him after a few months of game playing. Finally, when Poochie told me that he had another girlfriend, I lost contact with him. Next, she introduced me to the guy who would have the largest impact on my life.

His name was Steven Tyler Baker. Standing over six feet tall, Steven was Vincent's best friend and a complete character. Comical as hell, but not the best looking guy in the world. At first I wasn't interested at all in him, but he just happened to be down there just about every time I went to visit Poochie. Eventually, my mother caught on that I was visiting boys over Poochie's house, so I wasn't allowed to visit her without her being around. Something in me just said that I was not going to take this anymore. I started just leaving without permission at all. Sometimes I would leave after my summer job and not come back until the last bus ran at about ten o'clock. It infuriated my mother, but at first she didn't feel too bad about it because she had no idea that Poochie was covering for me when I saw Steven.

At first, I couldn't stand him. He was repulsive, a high school drop out, no job, still lived at home, the complete bottom of the barrel type of nigga. Not my type whatsoever. After catching the subway to his house one day after school, all these thoughts were popping through my head. I couldn't believe Poochie had set me up with somebody who was so not my type. I tried to let him down easy as we strolled through Druid Hill Park. During our walk together, I realized that although he was not my type of guy, I had never laughed so hard in my life than when I was with him.

He was the first guy I had been with who was not trying to paw me to death and who actually listened to me. When it began raining, he got a piece of newspaper and held it over my head so my hair wouldn't get wet. After that, I was hooked and in fantasy land. I was sneaking on the phone with him whenever I could get a chance. I would walk to the nearest shopping center just so I could use the payphone to call him. When my mother found out, I was forbidden to see Poochie at all now. But this time, I let those words go in one ear and out of the other.
I began the twelfth grade with the same attitude problems I had in the eleventh. Instead, this time, I had a steady boyfriend who I spent days with on the phone in school. We would talk on the phone at least two hours during the time that I was supposed to be in class. I was in puppy love and didn't care about school, religion, nothing but Steven. On the weekends I would sneak and see Steven not even thinking twice about getting caught or getting beatings. It was driving my mother crazy, because she didn't always know where I was. I would always catch the last bus back home and she would let me in. I would receive the mandatory beating with a belt. I was seventeen years old and all of us were still getting beatings on a regular basis although it was clear that this form of discipline was not working. I just led my own little life with no regard for how it was affecting anybody else.
My immediate plans for the future was (1) graduating from high school, (2) getting a job, (3) moving to Towson Maryland with Steven, and living happily ever after. I thought it was that simple, all I had to do was

wait until I graduated. I told myself that I hadn't gone through twelve years of high school just to drop out. That's all we did was talk on the phone, telling each other how much we couldn't wait to be together. I only saw him once or twice a month because it was getting harder and harder to convince my mother that I would leave him alone. When I wouldn't return at a certain time, the doors would be locked with no chance of getting back in. The last time I left, I had to spend the night on the Owings Mills subway bench because I had missed the last bus that would take me closer to my house. My mother refused to pick me up, so I snuggled up next to my jacket and tried to sleep.
It was not the first or the last time that I would spend the night outside, cold and alone. It was nothing to be brought back home by a routine police officer making his rounds. They would always tell my mother that legally, she couldn't just put us out on the streets, no matter what we did. They told her that she could have me declared incorrigible and I could be placed in a group home. If I was not almost eighteen at the time, there's a possibility that I could have spent time in a foster home or group home, just like my sisters.
Life at home was unbearable. My mother and I clashed 24/7 and Cocoa was now copying my example of leaving out. She had herself a boyfriend as well who lived in the city and as soon as I snuck out to leave, she would be going her own way right after me. Although I was not having sex, Cocoa certainly was and it was not long before she found out she was pregnant. She was only fourteen years old and her attitude about life and living at home was even fouler than mine. My mother was too ashamed to let her

continue school so it was decided that she would drop out at the end of the tenth grade. I was wrapped up in my own little world and all I cared about was spending time with Steven who continued to profess his love to me constantly.

After we had a huge argument over something petty, I just walked out of my classroom, begged on the street for bus fare to go see him and after collecting it, caught the subway over to his house. It was this night, on his basement floor when I had real sex for the first time. I got absolutely nothing out of it and I was left with the feeling of, is this it? I didn't think about protection or anything. I just got tired of waiting for it.

I ended up staying with Steven for about a week until his mother finally thought maybe it would be a good idea if I at least checked back home and let my mother know I was okay. I showed up one day after being gone all that time without her having any idea where I had been. I remember her sobbing angrily as she pummeled me with her fists. I can still see her tears of pain and frustration in dealing with a teenage daughter who just won't listen. Even after seeing all the hurt on her face, I would still defy her. A few days later, I was off to see Steven again. Nothing and nobody could keep us apart.

Chapter Eleven

Within a few days of being home after being gone for that entire week, I began to get a sense that I could be pregnant. I knew that even though we only had sex once, he had not used any protection. He swore he had pulled out but I had a funny feeling that that was not true. I started getting symptoms that I tried to ignore. I was more tired than usual, I found myself actually sleeping in my classes. Once, the teacher even had to wake me up. More importantly, I was late as late could be. I made an appointment at the Alpha Pregnancy Center for a free pregnancy test. I knew they would keep everything totally confidential. Despite my "gut feeling" that I was pregnant, I was shaken to find out that I was indeed six weeks pregnant. I knew exactly when I had conceived. When I found out I was pregnant, I decided right away that I was going to get an abortion. A baby was no where in my plans. I didn't even like kids, didn't have the patience for them, and didn't want kids. I was depressed and angry about everything. I certainly had no intention of telling my mother. When I told Steven, he was thrilled and wanted me to keep it but I refused. I kept telling myself that if I would ignore how I was feeling that it would all just go away. Maybe I would be lucky enough to have a miscarriage, I thought. I stayed miserable and depressed all of the time and fantasized about making all of this go away. I set up an appointment for an abortion but got discouraged when I found out how much it would cost. I found out that my health coverage would pay for it so I made the appointment with a local hospital. I even stole my mother's Blue Cross and Blue Shield health insurance card out of her wallet, not really knowing how insurance worked or what. What I didn't know was that Cocoa had known all along that I was pregnant from listening in on my phone calls with Steven. I had no idea that she had already told my mother I was pregnant. On the day of my appointment, my mother met me at the bus stop and demanded the insurance card back. That confirmed for me that she knew what I had been hiding for so long. I was stunned to see that she was not upset with me. She was almost pleased that I had screwed up royally. She knew the last thing I wanted was a baby. I had proven her right all these years that I wasn't nothing but a slut who wouldn't never amount to anything anyway. She got me my own private doctor and told me that I was not going to get an abortion. That was totally out of the question. She would do anything to help, but I was to finish school and raise the baby at home. I wasn't even hearing that because I truly didn't want to have kids. After pouring out my heart to Poochie once again, she allowed me to move in with her. She finally had her own place in the Po Homes Housing Projects and I knew that if I moved in with her, I wouldn't have the restrictions that I had at home. I eagerly agreed to move in with her in spite of my mother's disapproval. I came home one day and announced that I would be moving out. Nobody was surprised when I left. I was hardly home anyway. My mother always said that if I left I would not be allowed to take a single thing that I had not bought myself. Fortunately, I had spent my money well and I had enough clothes and things I would need for the time being. For the first time in my life, I would be living in a place where there were no rules. I would be responsible for myself. I could come and go as I pleased with no bullshit. I could spend as much time with Steven as I wanted. Just three months shy of my eighteenth birthday and impending graduation, I left with not a single goodbye to anyone, no regrets, no looking back.

Chapter Twelve

When I hooked up with Poochie I don't think I fully understood the conditions I would be living in. Poochie had her own two young children and another new boyfriend that was living with her as well. She was pregnant again with her third child. I was given this small cot with a thin, jail-like mattress to sleep on. I didn't really care as long as I could see Steven, who came over almost every day. Right away I was exposed to the way Poochie had been living. I was *initiated* to life in the projects, *"B-more"* style. Poochie's boyfriend Tony sold heroin out of her house so that they could make a little cash. Like Marlene, Poochie had picked up a heroin habit from one of her boyfriends. She also snorted a little cocaine on the side just *"to take the edge off"* she told me.
It seemed as though they both were born just to breed and to get high.
My first night living with her, I explained my problem to her about not wanting to be pregnant, and she made the suggestion that if I sniffed some dope then I would have a miscarriage. I had never even thought of trying to do heroin before. I vaguely even knew what it was, but since everyone who lived there was doing it, I

snorted a few lines, too. This sudden feeling of nausea immediately overwhelmed me. I just felt sick. I couldn't understand how everyone else around me seemed to be high as a kite but all I was doing was trying my best to keep from throwing up. That was the only time I tried heroin and the miscarriage didn't happen.

Poochie then had the idea that I use her medical assistance card to get the abortion. "You could just pretend that you're me." she suggested. I don't know why I hadn't thought of that before. When I made the appointment to go to Planned Parenthood to get it done, Steven begged me not to do this to him. Not even listening or even considering his feelings, I walked the ten blocks to the clinic. I expected that they would snatch this out of me right then and there. But it turned out that I was almost four months pregnant, and I would have to have at least two more appointments before the actual abortion could take place. By that time, the nurse told me, I would be about eighteen weeks pregnant. Plus they were suspicious as to why my medical records did not match up with who I was saying I was. Completely discouraged, I gave up on the idea of getting an abortion and just accepted that I was pregnant and there wasn't anything I could do about it. I sat on the bus stop, depressed, totally disgusted with myself.

I continued to go to school, by catching almost three buses and the subway to get to the county. I didn't have to pay a dime because my transportation was all paid for by MTA. I got preferential treatment because I was a pregnant senior with only two more months to go before graduation. All I had to do was continue going to school.

Since Poochie regularly sold her food stamps for cash for drugs, there was hardly ever any food in the house. I saw first hand what dope and coke had done to Poochie. She was addicted to both. She depended on a drug to get up and a drug to take her back down. She was gone. I mean *gone*. Unlike us, she didn't complain about starving. She thought a meal for her kids consisted of giving her eighteen month old daughter a bottle of formula and her son a pop tart. She thought it was a treat if she could come up with a hit of dope instead of food. Sometimes we survived solely on the milk, cheese, and cereal that Poochie got from her WIC vouchers. But when she found a way to make a few bucks selling these, we went back to starvation mode.

Have you ever felt what if feels like to be *really* starving? What you know about being so weak that you can barely get out of the bed to even go to the bathroom? All you do is try to sleep it off, minute by minute, hour by hour. I starved so much during my pregnancy that even at seven months pregnant, I was still able to wear my same clothes and had only gained ten pounds. I'm talking about hunger pains so powerful you're trembling with weakness and the only taste in your mouth is the taste of your own spit. There were times when I went to school just to receive my only meal of the day.

After going three days without anything but ice, ketchup, and instant oatmeal, I could barely hear the knocking on the door downstairs. I crawled to the front door to open it. Like an answer from God, Cocoa stood at the door. I hadn't even seen or heard from her since I left home.

"What happened to you?" she asks.

"Poochie's gone and left the kids here with me. These kids ain't had nothing to eat in three days. She do this shit all the time."

"Where's Steven?" she demanded.

"As soon as I know, I'll let you know."

Fattened with her pregnancy, I had not gained a pound and I was almost five months pregnant. In fact I was losing weight. She took pity on me, went to the nearest market with her food stamps. She filled the house with hotdogs, candy, cereal, milk. It was like Christmas in freaking May.

I soon realized that Poochie was getting high more than anyone had suspected. With no thoughts about her pregnancy, Poochie was snorting heroin and cocaine daily, like it was going out of style. I just left it all alone because Steven was very controlling over me and the child that I was carrying. He wouldn't even allow me to be around the stuff. He would send me to my room as if I was a child but join the others downstairs who were *"beaming up to Scotty"*. Soon, he had no choice but to admit that he "occasionally" sniffed dope to take the edge off. *The edge off of what, I thought?* The nigga didn't even work! Hell, everybody who came to the house would be zooted off of some drug.

I was left alone in that back room where I spent my time babysitting her kids and daydreaming about a future that I saw to be really fucked up. I'm pregnant with a kid that I don't really want, I'm living in the projects, sleeping on a cot where I have to fight the roaches off as if I'm competing with sleeping space. What kind of life is this? Even thoughts of Steven don't cheer me that much. I had no idea he was this deep into drugs. No wonder he was always so affectionate on the phone. No wonder he was so sleepy all the time. No wonder he was losing weight and throwing up for no apparent reason. I had been knocked up by a junkie and was too stupid to even see it coming.

Life in the projects was way different from life in Baltimore County. I remember the first time I heard gunshots, I was terrified as it woke me out of my sleep. Poochie said that I would get used to it. There was always somebody trying to buy drugs, sell drugs, or do drugs right at your door. There was always somebody selling blowjobs or stale pussy right outside of your door or around the corner. Once while I was walking to the store a body seemed to fall from the sky and landed at my feet. Turns out this guy was trying to kill himself by jumping out of a fifth floor window. Not only did he live, but was able to get up and walk away from the laughter that followed him from everybody who had just witnessed what happened. There was always something going on in the projects. Especially at night, is when it's really live. The Projects never shut down, business stays open 24/7.

My daily routine consisted of getting up at five in the morning, catching a bus to go downtown to the subway, riding the subway out to Owings Mills, and catching another bus to school. My grades were not anything to write home to Moms about. To explain away all my sleeping in class, my mother told my teachers that I was pregnant and now lived in the city.

They told me that the bottom line was that all I had to do to graduate with my class was to come to school every single day and to pass my final exams. It was a struggle to get up every morning and still go to school, after being up all night. My mother supported me one hundred percent. She paid for my cap and gown, graduation mug, everything, although I was still living with Poochie. She set me up for my first doctor's appointment when I was almost five months pregnant. I had not received any pre-natal care or anything for those first five months. Even when I received my sonogram picture showing that I did have a baby inside of me, I didn't feel any connection with this "thing" that wouldn't go away. I wanted no kids. Steven was thrilled and elated, but I was depressed and pissed off at the world. How in the world could I have managed to get pregnant the first time I got some from him? God, it was depressing! I was still hoping for a miscarriage or some miracle of some sort to take all of this away.

The only exciting thing I could look forward to was my graduation from high school. I was determined to do what everyone else said I wouldn't do. There was no way I had gone through twelve years of getting up early, just to throw it all away. I was gonna get that high school diploma even if it meant nothing to me but to show everybody who doubted me, that I would do this. I didn't see a high school diploma as the key to success in life anyway. It was just a piece of paper to me. I just wanted to prove everyone wrong who said I wouldn't make it. I had to prove my mother wrong. I had to prove my sisters wrong. On the night before my graduation, I was told that I wasn't welcome to stay at my mother's house while she was at work because I could not be trusted. Used to the "family routine" of limited association when someone moves out, I had no choice but to stay the night over my father's house. He unhesitatingly gave up his bed for me and slept on the couch. All night he kept telling me that, "of course, I'll be at your graduation." He told me how proud of me he was. I saw it as I had screwed up big time because I had managed to get pregnant, but he didn't see it that way at all. He kept telling me that I was the first in the family to do something positive and probably the only one to do so. He put it in my head that no matter what anyone said, he knew I would make it.

When I graduated, it was one of the happiest days in my life. I had proved that I would get my high school diploma no matter what. I walked across that stage, five months pregnant, jubilant as all hell while my parents and brothers and sisters sat in the audience and cheered me on. It was the best feeling in the world. I had received my diploma and was ready for what the world had to offer me.

Three days later, I applied for welfare.

Chapter Thirteen

I don't know how I didn't see it coming, but once I started getting my own money from a monthly welfare check, I began to notice subtle changes in Steven. He was more agitated, more stressed out. He wasn't working, was occasionally selling drugs on the side just to come visit me with forty dollars in his pocket. Sometimes he bought or stole us dinner and the best times spent with Steven was in those early days when I was myself one hundred percent and trusted him one hundred percent. It was the year 1990 and times were not so bad that we couldn't walk to the Safeway Market at Mount Clare Junction, sometimes two in the morning. Eight months pregnant and whatever he stole would be my only meal of the day. I was welcome at his home too, and I would sometimes spend nights over there. At one point, the times I spent with him were good.

Then from the time I got my first welfare check, I began to live the life of a battered woman. It's hard to even talk about today, because it went on for so long. In spite of being pregnant and helpless, I continued to stay with a man who had some serious mental problems upstairs. What's more, he was addicted to heroin, weed, and alcohol at the young age of eighteen. For some reason, I think I completely lost a grip on reality. I told myself that no matter what, I had to stay with this man because I was carrying his baby. That was my firm belief. I believed in loyalty because I felt that we were bonded together. I stayed no matter what.

Ask any battered woman who stuck with her man when she knew he was whipping her ass and she'll tell you that at some point she even believed that she was the cause of him acting this way. Especially if you are already young, weak-minded, and alone. There were times I had black eyes, busted all up, we fought like cats and dogs and this went on for years. And the worse thing about it was that I never knew when his rage would surface. Never knew when he would just snap. He always apologized after every episode and swore it would be his last. *"I just love you so much I just don't know how to show it,"* I would hear this bullshit constantly. Everybody in my family had a feeling of what was going on, but I would always deny it because of the shame I felt. It was a mess.

You see, I always believed that if only we could be together then everything would be all right. I was eight months pregnant when I was introduced to the *real* Steven. The first time he hit me, we were beefing over me not giving him ten dollars to buy drugs. I had been sitting there wondering why he was balling up a towel over his fist. I didn't even see it coming when he slammed his fist into my face. I screamed and instantly, his brother Tracy, his friend Vincent, and Poochie, were on top of him trying to pull him off of me. Surprised as fuck, I leaped on him and tried to literally beat the piss out of him. As if us coming to blows wasn't enough drama for one day, he told me something that hurt worse that any blow he could ever deliver.

He was saying he was sorry, so sorry over and over. "Well, since it's really over then, I might as well tell you everything." he sighs.

"Everything like what?"

"I had sex with your sister."

He says this all in one breath as if it's part of a normal conversation and we are just chatting about the weather or something. If he's really just trying to hurt me, this little game of "who can I hurt the most" is over. He tells me that he had sex with Poochie but only once. I don't buy this for one minute and I start to recall all the times when I came down and he was over here with her. Alone. I thought about her doing all of the things to him that I wouldn't do. I thought about all the promises of loyalty to me he had made and I ran out of the room, vomiting in the toilet. I called Poochie in my room to see if this was true and she said it was. She said, "I thought Steven was just a fling to you. I ain't really know he meant that much to you."

I could hardly believe what I was hearing. She knew that all I talked about was Steven this, Steven that. The whole time they had been fucking around right under my nose.

I can't even begin to describe how it feels when your heart is breaking into a million pieces. I was so sick with grief. It was like somebody had died. I thought that Poochie and I were so close, but I guess I was wrong. *In spite of it all, I stayed with him.* Moved out of Poochie's house and into his mother's home near

Druid Hill Park. I wouldn't even speak to Poochie for the next four years.

I think once he knew I forgave him for what he had done, he felt he could do practically anything to me and I would never leave him. He was hardly ever home and when he was, he was doped up more often than not. I was left in the house. Alone, reading books, depressed into oblivion.

When I clashed with his mother over something petty, I moved in with Marlene. The conditions at her house were even worse that Poochie's. Marlene was now totally crack addicted and her house stayed live with crackheads, 24/7. Pregnant with her fourth son, Marlene didn't even try hiding her drug use. This would be her third son born with crack cocaine in his blood. Everybody was still cramped in that hot ass two bedroom boiler room called a "project". Why they keep it so hot in the projects I'll never know. Steven would still visit me sometimes but Marlene was unbending in letting him in her house. She knew he had been beating on me and she couldn't stand the sight of him.

"It's hot as Hades in here. I'm sweating bullets, fanning myself for even a minimal amount of relief. My four nephews are running wildly throughout this hellhole of an apartment. Sleep is impossible with this racket so I clumsily walk to the rear of the apartment to get closer to the fan in the bedroom. As I'm walking through the hallway, I see that the door to Marlene's room is just slightly ajar. I watch her, sucking on her glass pipe like she is sucking juice out of a straw. Her face is contorted, her cheeks are almost touching each

*other she is sucking so hard. She's turning crimson
from the exertion. It is the first time I've ever
witnessed her getting high off of crack cocaine.
Mortified, when I realize what she is doing, I open the
door. Startled, she drops the pipe and it smashes into
glass crumbs on the floor. "Oh, I ain't see you come
in," she explains. She seems oblivious to my presence
as she drops to her knees to rescue whatever is left of
the drug. I pretend I don't see what is going on as I
back out of the room."*

I don't know what had happened to me emotionally but
I prayed for a release. My life was in total disarray. I
was eighteen, nine months pregnant, receiving a
welfare check, renting a room in the projects,
absolutely no plans for the future what so ever.
On October 21,1990 after an easy labor with Steven by
my side, my daughter was born into this world.
Although I had hated being pregnant, hated being in
labor, felt absolutely no connection to this child while I
was carrying her, all of that changed once I held her in
my arms. As I held my child in my arms I felt like *now
I was responsible for somebody else's life here*. I knew
I had to make changes in my life in order to do the best
I could do for her. *I had to be the one to do this*.
Silently, I promised her that I would do whatever it
took to provide the best life that I could for her.
Having a daughter gave me a purpose in life,
something to wake up to, something to focus on, a
sense of direction. Every choice I made now, I would
make for whatever was best for her.

Chapter Fourteen

I bought my daughter, Kendra back to the only place I
had to stay. Marlene's house again. As always, she
welcomed us with open arms. I felt like a whole new
person, full of responsibilities. I knew I had to make
some changes in my life, I just didn't have a clue on
where to start. Steven was full of promises of bettering
himself and getting clean to help take care of us, but I
knew he was full of it. I loved my daughter more than
I loved myself and I told her all the time that things
would get better for us.

After I saw this enormous rat scurrying across
Marlene's living room floor, I took that as my cue that
it was time to go. I begged my mother to let us stay
with her until I was able to save up for my own place.
Out of pity for my daughter, Kendra, she agreed to let
us stay until I got on my feet. As a bonus, she even
allowed me to continue to visit Steven on the
weekends. I guess she felt since I was over eighteen
now, I could not be easily controlled. Besides, I was
only staying there temporarily. I began to save up my
welfare checks to get enough money to move out on
my own. Steven was a little upset because he could no
longer see me as often as he was used to, but I felt that

we needed a break. Still addicted to heroin, we fought constantly about him getting and keeping a job. I hated depending on a monthly check and food stamps to make ends meet. He, on the other hand, seemed to be perfectly fine with it. He had no goals or plans for his life and we fought about it relentlessly. While I was visiting him at his home one day, his rage reared its ugly head once again.

We were arguing about something and I began to snatch my pictures off of his wall. The next thing I knew, we were wrestling on his bed. Once we came up for air, I kind of laughed at the irony of the situation. *We are sitting here fighting over something so dumb, I thought*. All of a sudden, **BAM!** He knocked me clear across the room, onto the floor. I literally saw sparks and cartoon characters, flying. Kendra was lying on the bed, watching us. Never in my life had I been hit that hard. I could almost feel the lump rising on the side of my head. Taken aback, all I could do was cry. "You said you wouldn't do this no more!" I sobbed. He apologized profusely over and over while holding me in his arms. Pissed to the point of no return, I gathered my things to leave. As I was limping down the street with my daughter on my hip, I uttered one final insult to him. I screamed, **"And you will never see your daughter again!"** All I saw next was his fist coming towards me. I didn't even feel the blows but before I hit the ground, he grabbed my daughter out of my arms. When I came to, he was lifting me off of the sidewalk and a small crowd had gathered around us. Through my swollen eyes, I could see blood on the sidewalk. It took a moment to realize that it was coming from my head. Among the faces I saw in the crowd were his aunt and his mother.

"Why Steven?" she asked.

He stammered, "Cause she play too many games."

He began the usual routine of accessing the damage and cleaning the blood off of my wounds. Tears streamed down his face as he apologized over and over. On the subway ride home, I ignored the stares of the passengers and cried softly to myself. I told my mother that I had fallen down the steps but she didn't buy that one bit. But since I wouldn't admit that he was beating on me, there was nothing she could do. I was covered with scars and bruises from head to toe. I remember limping up the stairs to a mirror to see just how bad I looked this time. I looked like someone who had been in a fight and lost. Both eyes swollen, head busted, cut lip, scars on my legs where I had fallen to the ground. I lifted my shirt and examined the boot prints on my back from where he had kicked me when I was out cold. I sat on the floor of the bathroom, hugged my knees, and cried. For some reason, I just couldn't even imagine a life without him. I so wanted him to be a part of my daughter's life that it was killing me inside. After a few days, I got tired of ignoring his repeated phone calls and began talking to him again.

Clashing with my mother over money, I took what little money I had saved up and finally moved to my own apartment on 2420 Madison Avenue. My first place wasn't too bad. It only had three rooms and the smallest kitchen in the world but I didn't care. It was all mine and I tried to make it a home. I told myself that maybe if we got our own place then he would relax, be a man, and get a job to help take care of us. I even started going to Cosmetology School to get a decent job. I let Steven move in with me on the condition that he was to get a job as soon as possible. But sure enough, things didn't quite turn out that way. Almost immediately, things went downhill once again. Steven couldn't stand the fact that I wanted to better myself to get a better job. He felt I should be satisfied with receiving a check and some food stamps. Hey, as long as it paid the bills, he was fine with it.

Just going to the Ron Thomas Cosmetology School began turning into a battle. He would hide my keys so I couldn't leave, or leave Kendra in the house so I couldn't leave without a babysitter. When I solved those problems by changing the locks and getting a babysitter free of charge through social services, he was furious. Finally, on one morning, I woke to find out that he had ripped out all the pages in the books I was studying, and cut all the hair off of my mannequin. Ultimately, I just gave up and dropped out of school. I told myself that I really didn't want to go to school for something I had no interest in anyway.

"I am crouched in the corner, hugging my knees, rocking back and forth. Steven is ranting and raving and throwing shit around. I know better to even open my mouth to say anything when he is like this. Earlier, I realize he is about to lose it cause he comes stumbling in and dumps all of Kendra's coins from her piggybank onto the bed. Pissed beyond belief, I snatch the bank out his hand and try to gather the quarters, nickels, dimes, that are scattered about. This escalates into an all out brawl where he ends up tossing me

against the wall. Once again, I run outside and almost, just almost, make it to the payphone on Whitelock Street. Now, he has just dragged me by my hair back into the apartment. When I don't act scared enough, he picks up a steel trashcan. I duck too late as it comes crashing down on the top of my head. As I hit the floor, I feel the toe of his boot coming in direct contact with my mouth. I taste the blood as I try to crawl away. It's funny how this hurts but it doesn't hurt. I am beginning to be immune to pain. My tolerance for pain is growing higher and higher. Kendra is practicing standing up in her playpen. My little angel is getting so big, I think. I force myself to concentrate on her. Concentrate on what I'm going to have for dinner, or what I'm going to wear tomorrow. Anything but the reason why I am laid up on this floor like this. I refuse to cry to give him the satisfaction of seeing that he has me scared senseless. He senses my anger simmering like a teakettle. I stare at him with all the hate I can muster, ever defiant, if only with my eyes. "Oh you think you bad, don't you? Come here, bitch!" He drags me across the floor and slams my head against the front door. Somehow, I manage to claw his face. His friend, Martin, finally has a little pity on me and convinces Steven to stop. He kicks me, one last time, on my side this time, in case I had any thoughts of leaving. I pretend I am watching this happen to somebody else. When I hear him laughing and joking with Martin outside, I survey the damage in the bathroom mirror as usual. This is becoming an everyday occurrence, I think to myself. How many times was it last week when I stood in this exact same spot, stared into this mirror and told myself that he swore on his grandmother's grave that this would be the last time? I can still feel the burning of my tears as they roll down my cheeks. How much longer can I put up with this? He doesn't even bother to apologize for this no more. He'll just come in, sit on the bed, sigh as if to say, "Oh I'm so sorry I did this." "Come here, let me take a look at you," he'll say. Wasn't it just the other day when he clocked me just for "breathing too loud?" After he cools off, he returns. This time he really swears this won't happen again and begins to help clear my face of the blood and tears. I actually keep a washcloth in the bathroom that is used just for the sole purpose of washing my wounds. "I just love you so much, I don't know how to show it," he sobs. It's his favorite saying and I finish it before he does. I know the routine by heart now. He shakes his head and looks down. His eyes are dripping with tears and his nose is running with snot. A part of me believes that he is really sincere this time, he only hits me because he doesn't know how to show his affection for me. Then again, parts of me want to just slit my wrist and die along with my sanity on this bathroom floor.

I called the police so many times, but they would always tell him to go cool off somewhere. This was before the "O.J. Simpson crises" and Baltimore City Police were not as hip to domestic violence as they are now. Plus, I really didn't want him to go to jail, I admit. But after one particular fight, I changed my mind. Leaving Kendra in the house, I jumped on the nearest bus I could find to get away from him. I rode the number twenty three bus all the way out to Cherry Hill and back. I thought to myself that I had to get out of this situation or he was going to kill me. It was that simple. I was only eighteen, I had a baby that I had promised to make the best life for her and I wasn't keeping my end of the deal. I had to get away. I expected an all out brawl when I returned, but was shocked to see that my front door was left wide open. When I walked into the apartment, the first thing I saw was Kendra standing up in her crib. She had finally learned to stand up on her own. Steven was nowhere to be found. That was the last straw for me. How could he have left her alone in the apartment for who knows how long? I finally confessed to my mother and father what had been happening to me for the past two years. My mother agreed to let me come back home, provided I would try to find somewhere else to live in the meantime. I also had to formally press charges against him, which I had no problem with doing. The next day, my father picked me up along with all my stuff and I left 2420 Madison Avenue. I had lived there only three months but it was three months of pure hell. I told myself that things just had to get better than this.

Chapter Fifteen

It was the end 1991. With the help of my parents, I was able to move into my very own apartment in upper Edmondson Village. A far cry from where I had been living. After years of struggling to find a place to stay on my own, I had finally succeeded. I had struggled with Section Eight programs, Housing Authority programs for the city and for the county. All without receiving any kind of real housing. I gazed around at the new kitchen counter, refrigerator, oven. I was awestruck with the central AC. I was so blessed with all utilities included. It even had a security door where you had to be manually buzzed in. With a playground out back for Kendra, I couldn't ask for more. The only downside was the rent was more than my monthly check. Fortunately, my mother and I came up with the agreement that I would sell her some of my food stamps to make up the difference. In addition, she would also purchase a monthly bus pass for me to help me look for a job. I was truly grateful for her help and began visiting home more and more. I guess we got along fairly well as long as we weren't living together. Besides, she was especially close to my daughter.

I worried about what to do with my future. I knew I didn't want to be one of those types of mothers who sits on their fat asses all day, watching soap operas, and collecting a check every month for years. I wanted my daughter to have only the best. All the things that I didn't have growing up. My very first job after high school was Subway in Mondawmin Mall. The pay was so cheesy that I was paid cash out of the register. Still believing in the "right thing to do", I allowed Steven to visit occasionally to baby-sit Kendra while I went to work. That job lasted only a few months and I hit the pavement again, looking for a job.

"I'm sitting on the couch, waiting. Waiting for Steven to calm down. Usually if I sit here quiet and still, he calms down and stops tearing apart things. But it's not working this time. He has just read my most intimate thoughts that was in my journal, tucked away under my mattress. I know he read the part about me going to see Antoine. It doesn't matter that I was only visiting him because he had been shot and was laid up in the hospital, asking for me. Steven's completely livid about this, despite the fact that I keep emphasizing we're no longer a couple. He says it's not over until he says it's over. Hoping he calms down, I am sitting here, not saying a word. He has the nerve to be pulling this shit right in my own house and this bastard doesn't even live here.

"Where was my daughter when you went to see this nigga? I know you ain't take my daughter over there!" he yells.

When I don't answer, he grabs me by my neck and with one hand, lifts me off the couch like a rag doll. He drags me over to my daughter, yelling all the while, "See? Your mother ain't shit! Your mother ain't shit!" Like lasers, my eyes scan to a hammer on the kitchen table. Flashes of me cracking his skull with it creeps in my head. Before I have a chance to react, the fight takes a more deadly tone. He wraps his fists around my hair and slams my head onto my glass dining room table, shattering it. I'm screaming my head off now, swinging blindly at him. He's on top of me with both hands around my neck, squeezing. Gasping for air, I'm clawing his face, his hands.

"I'm going to fuck you up so bad ain't nobody gonna want you."

He grabs the scissors off the table and begins snipping my hair. Somehow, I make it off the floor and out the front door. I'm running, barefoot, in the darkness outside. Clad only in my nightgown, I'm banging on my neighbors doors, screaming for help. An elderly woman finally lets me in, allows me to use her phone. Frantic, I call 911. I thank her profusely over and over, while glancing behind me to see if he's coming for me. I'm practically incoherent when the police show up. They escort me back to my apartment. Steven is nowhere to be found, but my apartment is left in shambles. Glass from the table is on the floor, blood is on the steps, dishes are broken, food and cereal boxes are thrown everywhere, my mattress is sliced up. Kendra is asleep in her crib totally oblivious to the mayhem out in the living room.

Later, at the hospital, I'm treated for a concussion and various cuts and bruises. This is it, I tell myself. I've totally had it. I'm completely drained of any emotion.

I don't feel safe until the police tell me that he has been arrested finally. Sentenced to 18 months in prison, he is long gone as I begin to rebuild my life."

Still unable to find a job with just a high school diploma under my belt, I realized that the only way I was going to get a halfway descent job was if I picked up a trade or went back to school to further my education. A high school diploma just wasn't gonna cut it. I began attending PTC Career Institute in downtown Baltimore, where I studied courses in Security and Investigations. I've always had an interest in forensics, the criminal justice system, and why people commit crimes. I was so proud of myself when I passed all my classes and received many awards of merits. But I was highly disappointed when after I completed all my classes, I found out the really good security investigator jobs had an age requirement of at least twenty one. I had just turned twenty and I was expecting to be able to work right away. Luckily, after a few months, I picked up a job where I would be working as a security officer for an apartment building. It was on the night shift, which was kind of a hassle, but I took it because I needed a job like yesterday. I actually liked the position where I was responsible for checking the grounds and maintaining logs. I began feeling better about myself now that I had a job and was living comfortably. I was single and had even begun attending meetings again at the Kingdom Hall. I felt I had to do all the right things for my daughter. It was at one of these meetings where I would meet a guy who would have another major impact on my life.

Allow me to be blunt for a minute, he was the finest nigga I had ever seen, in the flesh. *(And anybody who knows me well, knows that my one weakness is pretty boys with big sticks.)* He was a dead ringer for Ginuwine, the singer. As cute and sexy as he wanted to be. It had been years since I had even been in a Kingdom Hall, and I had expected things to be as I had left them. But I soon found out that was not so. I wasn't the young kid who was used to sitting in the front row at all the meetings, raising my hand to answer all the questions. Now, I was petite, only five feet two inches I stood. Long hair, light skinned, sporting 36D's, the works. I was never the type of girl to just approach a guy, so I waited and waited for him to approach me, as I knew he would. Even if it was only to say what's up. I knew he would at least say *something* to me. It took him about two weeks. He lived only a few blocks away from my apartment and I would see him a lot as I waited on the bus stop to go to school, driving his rimmed out Toyota Cressida. He would step to me in ways that I didn't think were too kosher for a Jehovah Witness. After we ended up giving each other massages one night, I caught on to his game in a bad way. I figured it out that he led two different lives. For some reason, I decided to play along right with him. Maybe pretty boys with weird minds were my weakness because gradually we started an affair that would last for over two years. Two long, lust filled years. I just felt drawn to him, somehow. In the Kingdom Hall, we were perfect saints who lead responsible, respectable lives. But after hours, late at night, he would be at my place, in my bed, rocking my mind.

"It's late. Past midnight and I am alone. And I can't sleep. And I'm lonely. Other than the sound of my daughter's breathing, it's quiet. In the darkness, I get out of bed. I reach for the phone and dial his pager number. I put my code in and pace around the bed, anxiously waiting for him to call me back. Fortunately, within a few minutes, he calls back. He knows exactly why I'm calling. No small talk as I offer him all I have. Sixty bucks. He says he can be over in about an hour and a half. He orders me to be ready. That means I must answer the door butt-ass naked. Before he arrives, I chase all the negative thoughts of what I am doing out of my head. Fuck it, it ain't no room for quilt or shame. I look forward to his arrival by spraying my sheets with his favorite perfume and dimming the lights. I lay my sleeping daughter on the couch in the living room. With Jodeci playing in the background, I wait by the window, wrapped in a sheet, until he arrives. When he rings my doorbell, surprisingly on time, we don't waste much time on chit chat. I tell him the money is on the TV. He pockets it and orders me to drop the sheet that I am covering myself with. Instead, I wrap the sheet around the both of us. He orders me to beg for it. I beg for it. He orders me to undress him. I undress him. Somehow I tell myself, that's this is easier to pretend that I am enjoying this. It's easier to pretend that this is a scene from a movie that I am watching, not my real life. I tell myself that I am only playing a role. I separate my mind from my body, totally. My mind is a thousand miles away as he thrusts into me, giving me what he's known for, good at."

Ron was like a force. Something I wasn't even used to and didn't know how to control. A force I had never experienced before and wasn't prepared for. I bet he never even knew how screwing around with him would affect me the way it did. He had my mind in the palm of his hands and had me doing things I never thought I would do. It was a self-discovery affair where this nigga had total mind control over me. He controlled my every move like a puppet dangling from a string. I had never met somebody who could lead two entirely different lives. I was so fascinated by him that I wanted to be with him, needed to be with him, 24/7, all the time. I mean, I needed him so bad I used to *pay* him to be with me. I got a better paying job just to support him. This wasn't even a relationship where we pretended to even care about each other. It was a strictly, sexual explorative, type of deal. He took me to places I had never been before, sexually and emotionally. *Steven was a snack, but Ron was a five-course meal with all the trimmings including dessert.* And I feened for him like a crackhead needing a hit. Sometimes I would feel bad about how I was totally deceiving the people at the Kingdom Hall, but the attraction to him were too strong. Too strong. He had the freakiest, weirdest type of mind that was a constant turn on for me. Ron had me doing practically anything for him. I paid his bills, bought his clothes, let him stay with me, bought his food, was his sex slave, you name it, I was there. The only thing I asked of him was to spend his time with me. I almost felt like it was a privilege to be in his company. I was always broke because I would end up paying his bills before mine. I was always giving him money for something that he just *had* to have. I don't know how I had sunk to a new low after managing to escape from Steven. Even Steven couldn't stop me from seeing him. Released from prison six months early, he returned to find me a whole new, different person. Ron eventually scared him off. Now I was with a nigga who I had to pay to fuck with me. He was like a drug that I didn't know how to get out of my system.

"I push him off of me. Surprised, he asks, "What's wrong?" I don't answer as I get up out the bed. I wrap the sheet around me and head to the bathroom. When I pass the mirror by the sink, I make eye contact with my own reflection. A voice in my head says harshly, "What are you doing? Just what the hell are you doing? You are sharing your bed with a man that you have to pay to spend time with you. "I stand there staring at the mirror as the "voice" continues. "You are letting him sleep with other bitches in your bed, screwing anybody he tells you to. What the fuck is wrong with you? How the hell did you stoop so low?" I rinse cold water on my face, drift to my living room window. I stare at my daughter, asleep on the couch as usual. I can't do this anymore. I can't let him control me like this anymore. I feel lower with him than I ever did with Steven. I have no "self" with him. Everything is a role, like a script from a porno flick. Loneliness has completely wracked my senses. What have I turned into, I ask myself? I'm so scared to face the truth. I don't even know who I am anymore. I've been running from myself for so long, I've lost me. My hands clasped together tightly, I plead to God, any God that will listen. Please help me to gain some

control over my life. Please help me to be able to look in a mirror and not be ashamed of what I see staring back at me. Help me to like me, at least once in my life. Please help me to find myself again. Please help me to find me again."

That very next day, I finally confessed to the Elders in the congregation what I had been doing. I told them all, (including his father) about all the illicit sex, the abortions. It was the hardest thing I've ever had to do because I had to confess, in detail, some of the most intimate moments in my life. It wasn't easy describing to his father how his *"ministerial servant"* son had just left my house last night. It wasn't easy but I knew that the only way for sure that I could get him out of my life was if I told the Elders in the congregation what I had been doing all these years. I knew he would hate me over that. Needless to say, they were shocked and didn't exactly welcome me with open arms. It was so hard to sit there and pour out my soul to a bunch of grown men who I felt absolutely no connection with. I was punished by an announcement from the platform that I would be on *"public reproof"*.
For years I held a grudge against him for the way he had treated me. But I had to ask myself, why? How could I blame him? I had chosen to live that type of lifestyle. It wasn't like he put a gun to my head and forced me to do all those things. Even though I was ashamed, I was relieved to have finally unloaded what had been killing me for so long. I was completely sorry and remorseful for what I had done. Looking back on the things that I did, it all made me a better person, a better wife.

Committee meetings with the elders are supposed to be confidential and that was what my beliefs were when I confessed everything to the elders. However, that was not the case with me. Within days, I could feel the stares from the people in the hall. I ignored the whispers at the conventions. I felt totally isolated and alienated at the Kingdom Hall and eventually I stopped going all together.

Just when I had given up on guys for good and was contemplating being a nun, I met Jamal. We started out as being strictly friends, but we soon discovered that we had a lot in common. Jamal was the first man I met who wanted to be around me just for who I was. I had finally met a man who loved me for me. A man who I could laugh with, cry with. And I finally met a man who fit the true definition of the word *man*. He put his family first, was hard working, treated my daughter like his own, and truly loved me. I knew he was going to be the man that I would marry. We fell in love, (me, for the first time) and I began to finally feel what true happiness feels like. He taught me how to love and be loved. He didn't care about what I had done in the past. Most importantly, my daughter loved him and he felt the same for her.

To get away from it all at the Kingdom Hall, I quickly moved into his place with him. Shortly after, I started a job with the Department Of Corrections at the Maryland Penitentiary. Things were looking up for me both financially and emotionally. I wanted to let everyone know that I was finally in love and made plans for Jamal to meet every one in my family. I was on cloud nine.

Chapter Sixteen

My family didn't fare as well as I did, though.
Marlene, now living on Baltimore's East Side, was
struggling with crack cocaine and heroin addiction.
With 5 boys to raise alone, to say life was hard for her
would be the understatement of the year. My nephews
were exposed to all types of physical and emotional
abuse. Marlene would beat them with anything she
could get her hands on. Sometimes they were left
alone in the house for hours at a time. The neighbors
and my mother called the Department Of Social
Services on her so many times that I'm sure they knew
her by name. Unable to care for them properly, the
Department of Social Services finally intervened and
removed them from her custody. She dissolved into
the clutches of drug addiction in Baltimore.
You see, Marlene had developed this cold, uncaring
attitude she picked up from years of hard living on the
streets of Baltimore. The only thing she cared about
was her next hit. She lost all contact with her five
sons. Only at her funeral, years later, were they
reunited. By that time, only her two oldest sons even
recognized or remembered her.

Poochie's apartment in the projects had finally been raided one time too many and she was placed on the Northwest side of Baltimore in the low income tenant units of Druid Park Lake Drive Apartments. She now had 4 kids and one on the way. All were by different men who were no longer around. She spent her days sleeping and her nights getting high off of crack cocaine and heroin. Eventually, she followed Marlene's example and gave her kids up to the foster care system. Once she was diagnosed with AIDS, she began to view life as just one more day to get high. Cocoa, now with three children, lived with Poochie and survived on welfare. She was also addicted to heroin and crack cocaine. She told herself that "as long as I'm not as bad as Poochie and Marlene, I'm fine."

Roshell had the most amazing story of them all. After she dropped out of high school in the eleventh grade, she moved in with an abusive boyfriend. She wasn't allowed to keep in contact with her family what so ever and we didn't see or hear from her for a number of years. She completely abandoned the family. For a while, we didn't even know where she was. She wrestled with her own demons.

There was so much backstabbing and deceit in this family that it was nothing new for somebody to change his or her address and not tell anybody anything. I have been in terrible fistfights with at least two of my sisters because of the he say she say. So when Roshell vanished for all those years, I envied the fact that she could just up and disappear and nobody knew where she was.

My two brothers had morphed into petty drug dealers. They did work regular jobs from time to time, but the majority of the time, they earned their cash by working the streets of Baltimore's drug trade. PJ. was the second and last of us to graduate high school. Like myself, he chose not to pursue a career in anything. Kenneth dropped out in the tenth grade and my mother didn't really protest the issue.

My mother finally began divorce proceedings with my father. Down on her luck and evicted from her home for the second time, she also moved in with Poochie to get a new lease on life and because she had no where else to go. I would visit her often and we developed the mother/daughter relationship I always wanted. She had been going to the hall faithfully all this time, but financial and personal woes were taking its toll on her. She started missing a few meetings here and there and eventually stopped going altogether.

I began to understand that there was a life out there for me somewhere, after high school. I just had to figure out what it is that I wanted to do. After years of no direction and no particular course of action to follow, I had to carve out my little niche in society. And I was going to have fun doing it. It was during this time that I was the happiest. Jamal and I spent all of our time together, raising my daughter, and making plans for the future. I was experiencing happiness at it's fullest. Jamal had already met most of my family members and I was eager for him to finally meet my father. I had not spoken with him in a while and was just beginning to bridge the gap between us after all of these years. I wanted to show him that I could be a major player in this game of life, I wanted him to be proud of me. Hopefully, we could establish a more meaningful relationship.

Chapter Seventeen

My father was murdered less than a year after I met Jamal. Parts of my life are a complete blur after the initial shock wore off. After his funeral, I found it increasingly hard to just put what had happened out of my mind. I thought about it all the time, everyday. I governed my life around what had happened to him. It was almost as if I had lost two parents, because two weeks after he was killed, my mother announced to the family that she, along with my brother, would be moving to North Carolina. I swallowed the feelings of doubt that were forming in my head about her involvement in his death. I wanted to find out who murdered him more than anything, but I wasn't sure if I was ready for the truth or not. From day one, I had feelings that maybe my mother knew more than what she was saying. It was common knowledge that she did detest him more than anyone I knew, she did benefit from his death more than anyone, they were going through a divorce. I found these thoughts to be unbearable. I didn't want to have her sent away for the rest of her life, but at the same time, I longed to find out who had killed him and why.

Losing my father to a crime where he was beaten almost unrecognizable devastated me to my entire being. I felt all the normal feelings of grief. *If only* I had of gone over there that night, *if only* this *if only* that. For months, I couldn't even sleep with the lights off because I kept seeing him in my dreams, calling for me. I felt that I had given up on him by not coming to visit him that night, I didn't even call to say that I wouldn't be showing up. I told myself that I would not give up on him this time. *I would stop at nothing to find out who did this to him.*

I began to keep in contact with the many detectives who have handled this case. After the case was passed around from detective to detective, it finally ended up with the cold case squad where it sat collecting dust for the next seven years. During those seven years the file just sat, I began to launch a one-woman crusade to help find his killer. I figured the best way to do that was to let the detectives know that I wasn't going anywhere and I was going to do what I could in getting this case solved. Every year on Father's Day and the anniversary of his death, I would call the detectives to find out if there had been a break in the case or anything, As always, there never was. I visited the detectives and gave a few taped statements implicating my mother in his death. It was always hard for me to tell them what I had suspected, but I couldn't live with the thought that he was murdered by someone who was supposed to have cared. For seven long years, I suffered in silence. I hid the pain by isolating myself from my family and writing about everything I was feeling in my journal. I kept telling myself that *somebody* killed him. *Why?* I was alone in this. I just couldn't understand why I was the only one who felt that strongly about what had happened to him. Everyone in the family had the idea that she could be involved, but they felt that he was better off dead. He was just a junkie who was never there for us anyway, they felt. We always felt that he was going to die from a drug overdose or something, never from somebody beating him to death. I felt like the biggest outsider. Despite his problems, he was a well-liked guy who had no enemies. Nobody on his job could say one bad word about him. And despite what I tried to force myself into believing, I couldn't get the idea out of my head that my mother had something to do with his murder. No matter how hard I wanted to believe otherwise.

(journal excerpts)

<u>Saturday, April 3, 1999</u>
"Sometimes I wish I was never born. I wish I could either go back in time or fast forward to the future. Anywhere but the present. I wish I had the courage to do what I know needs to be done. I'm trying so hard to focus on me and my life so much I'm exhausting myself. There's so many things that are wrong with my life that I don't know how to fix them. It would be cool if I could just talk to Mom about what has been tearing my brain apart for so long. But she's part of the problem. Why won't she talk to me? Why? I really need to find out what's wrong with me and why I can't even plant a fake smile on my face. Why am I constantly depressed? I should be happy that I have a

new house, my dream car, wonderful kids, and a loving husband. Why am I not happy?"

It happened so gradually. I had experimented with weed before with Steven but it never worked. I just didn't like it. And other than the previous experience I had had with the heroin, I never did drugs. I didn't even drink, really. But one day in 1997 I was introduced to weed the right way and I felt something totally different within a few minutes. A total feeling of *no worries* crept over me. My senses were alerted to the fifth degree. I mean I could smell the grape Kool-Aid that somebody was making next door. I could hear birds singing at midnight. I had never felt so relaxed in my life. It was as if all my problems were manageable. I could dream when I was high as a kite. The feeling was way better than the depressing feeling of drinking forties. I depended only on weed. I couldn't function without it. It helped me to relax; it helped me to cope. It elevated my mind. This is not an ode to weed, because although I did get lifted on a regular basis, I suffered tremendous guilt over it. I began to hate myself for doing it. I would stay sober for about a month out of the year and be fucked up for the following eleven months.

(excerpts from my journal)

<u>Sunday, August 15, 1999</u>
"I am becoming addicted to weed. Can you believe this shit?! Weed makes me feel so relaxed. It helps me to cope with everything that has been on my mind. Honestly, I tell myself that weed is not that bad. Hey,

it's safer than alcohol or heroin and I swear, everybody's doing it. It sort of makes me forget my problems and sometimes gives me the confidence that I need. But when the weed is all gone, those problems are still there, staring at me with a vengeance. I've smoked so much weed I hardly have any air in my lungs anymore. Sometimes when I go to sleep fucked up with my heart racing and tightening in my chest, I actually pray that I die in my sleep. Just let me drift here and not wake up. Then I think about my kids and the thought of someone else raising them and I want to hang on just a little bit longer. This morning I fantasized about killing myself, taking sleeping pills or stopping up the exhaust pipe on my car. Just drifting into a deep, deep sleep and never waking up. It's a shame that the only reason I stay alive is because of my two kids. I couldn't stand the thought of Kendra or Jason being raised by someone else. For those reasons alone, I continue to exist. It's been four years and I still think about Daddy everyday like it was just yesterday that he was killed. I actually ache with grief sometimes. I wish I could just see or talk to him one more time. And what makes it worse is I know in my heart, Mama had something to do with it. And I still love her. The things I need for her to say to me, she never will. Did she know that she would intentionally screw up all of our lives? I don't think so. My prayers are getting better. I pray to a God who I'm not even sure hears me. Even though I was raised extensively to believe there is a God, I can't yet grasp the idea that God listens to me. I have sinned so much against Him that I could be the anti-Christ. From abortions to addictions, how could I possible believe that I can be forgiven after all that I have done? I have totally reached rock bottom. I am praying, sweating, dreaming, aching for God to help me out of this mess of a life."

Weed became like my best friend. I think the lowest I got, to be really honest, was pretty low for somebody of my standards. I used to be a *"poster child"* for *"say no to drugs"*. I saw from experience what drugs can do to a person's life. It destroyed my sisters, it destroyed my father, everywhere around me there were drug addicts. And yet still, how did I succumb to weed? I didn't even want to use the word "addiction" because it's such an ugly word. But it came to the point where I couldn't go thirty days without weed. It wasn't hard to get, everybody was doing it. It was almost like where it wasn't even a drug. It was glorified everywhere. And no, weed isn't crack, cocaine, or heroin, but it's still a drug. A substance that I abused every chance I got. I mean, it was nothing for me to smoke like three blunts in one day. I had blunts for breakfast, lunch, and dinner. And two sleeping pills for desert. And this went on for years. As I smoked and drove in traffic, I prayed that if I got in an accident, it would be quick. Life was too hard anyway. I didn't fear death what so ever because I felt that I was living a hell on earth anyway. I felt like shit 24/7 with no type of self-esteem. I was drowning in marihuana smoke laced with sleeping pills. I didn't even realize I was out of control until one day I looked at my collection of calendars that I have and read about it in my journal. It dawned on me that I had been smoking everyday for almost four years straight. I told myself that if I could just get a grip on whatever was

making me do this, then I could stop. The problem
was I stayed fucked up so much that I didn't even
know what was bothering me anymore. Maybe if I
could just find a reason to be happy. I was
accomplishing everything that I wanted to do in life yet
I hated myself, hated everything about my life and I
didn't know why.
I became obsessed with memories that would connect
me to my childhood. My father loved music and I
actually started a Mobile Disc Jockey service just
because it was something that I loved to do and it made
me think of him. I collected old school music that
nobody else was playing in the clubs. I was making a
suitable amount of income doing so. Almost every
move I made in my life was a reflection of him and
what I figured he would want me to do. I could always
see him encouraging me, and that's how I made it
through the really rough times. I swear I wanted to get
close to my mother but I could only get *so close.* I
knew that his murder had changed us, I knew that the
only way we could even began to get close was if I
knew for sure she was not involved in his murder.
I tried to do everything I could to bring some joy to my
life. I got married, I bought a house, I got my dream
car, even started two profitable businesses and I still
was a walking time bomb. I thought I would be
happier if I accomplished these things. But I still
couldn't sleep at night. I tried to talk to Mama about
what I was feeling, even tried to get her drunk enough
to talk about him. But she would always change the
subject, would always deny any involvement, would
tell me to just get over it. In the meantime, I'm dying
for some answers, some closure. I'm visiting her in
North Carolina trying my best to develop a relationship

with her. Needing, wanting the affection from her that I need and there's a wall between us that I have to knock down once and for all. His murder and her possible involvement truly affected my life. It affected the type of mother and wife I was becoming. I couldn't just "get over it" like she insisted that I do. I would see other people with their father's or grandfathers and I would stay depressed for weeks. I would see how people interacted with their mothers and I would cry silently because in a way, I felt that I had lost her, too. It came to a point when my husband finally just mentioned that I may have to just accept that his murder will never be solved. And I knew that I couldn't do that. I just couldn't. I told myself constantly that I had to put this episode behind me. I had to find out the truth even if it killed me. In my letter that I wrote to Sergeant Roland, I begged them to at least bring her in for questioning. I begged them to at least rule out the possibility that she was involved. I begged them to at least do something. But no response. I felt trapped, frustrated, and alone. I had to do something.

Dear Mom,
I have to tell you that I am really glad you wrote me this time because I would never have the courage to tell you this on the phone or face to face. I'm really glad that you are getting your life right with Jehovah. Hopefully, that will help you to feel better about yourself and find real happiness. My life has dwindled into me taking sleeping pills in order to fall asleep at night. Me smoking weed just to be able to go on another day. I literally hate myself and the type of person I am becoming. Mom, I say this to finally

confront you with what is ruining me. Mom, I never got over Daddy's murder. It stays with me constantly. Not a day goes by that I don't think about what happened to him and it's tearing me apart. It has been seven long years and I long to find out what happened to him and why it happened. Ever since I found out about him being killed, I have always had this feeling that you had something to do with it. It hurts me to the core of my entire being to even say that, but it's how I feel. Even though I felt like this for so long, I still loved you. If I am wrong, I swear I would understand if you hated me for the rest of you life and wouldn't have anything to do with me anymore. If I am wrong, please forgive me. I just wanted you to know how life really is for me. I could lie and pretend that everything is okay, but it's not and it has not been for years. I just know that I honestly feel like I can not move on with whatever life I do have left until this is solved. I can't help but feel that Daddy knew somehow that I was supposed to be over there. I know it sounds stupid but it's how I feel. And I'm not ever going to stop pursuing his case because who else is? He has to know that somebody did care. If that was you murdered, I would not stop at anything to try to have it solved. If you did not have anything to do with this, please make me believe that. Make me believe that I am totally going crazy and I have blamed you for something so terrible that you won't even accept my constant apologies. Please make me believe that this is not true.

Your daughter,
Tia

Chapter Eighteen

Sergeant Roland,

On February 25, 1995 my father Leroy Lincoln was brutally killed in his own home. Monday will be seven years of grief his death has caused for me. For seven years I have not been fully able to move on with my life. I am constantly depressed, sad, and miserable. This has affected my marriage of five years. I have always blamed myself for his death because you see, I was supposed to introduce him to my fiance that night. Sometimes in my sleep I can still see him lying there bleeding to death, waiting for me to arrive. Even after seven years I still ache with grief. I still tear up at the mention of his name. I still find myself sad and depressed every Father's Day or towards the end of February. My father was a real person. Yes he had his problems with drugs. But I am one hundred percent convinced that his murder was not drug related in any way. From the night Detective Carter came to my home and informed me of his murder, I have always implicated my mother in his death. I still believe and know that it's true. I beg you to please reopen this case. In 1996, 1998, and 1999 I gave complete, taped statements and I would be happy to do so again. I know that a lot of hard to solve cases have been solved with the use of DNA. Can this somehow be applied to my father? Right after his murder my mother moved to North Carolina and she rarely visits. Now for fear of being questioned by detectives, I have not even heard from her in months which is not normal. Although she has never confessed to me, her actions, her words, show that she knows something. I have always felt that she, along with my brother, should have at least been questioned. She had all the actions someone planning a murder would have. Why was she never questioned? I beg you once again to reopen this case, please, so I can have some closure to this, finally. I still love my mother dearly, but I am having the hard task of just accepting that she actually got away with this. Maybe there is a slim chance that she didn't have anything to do with this. If so, can DNA rule this out? My father had no known enemies except the one who was divorcing him and hated him more than anything.

Thank you for your time,
Tia L. Whitehead

P.S.   I can be contacted for anything at the numbers listed below. Please do not hesitate to call me or to just let me know that this letter was read by someone.

It's hard for an outsider, a person who is not from Baltimore to really understand how living in Baltimore really is. Baltimore to me, is like another world, separate from all other major hard-core cities. I've lived here all my life from the streets of North Avenue to the West side of Park Heights. I've lived in the worse of Baltimore City from the high rises of Lexington Terrace to the slums of Madison Avenue. I've lived in it all and most outsiders usually ask me is Baltimore really that violent? Is there really at least *a murder a day* in Baltimore? Is Baltimore really that bad? My answer is, *yes it is*. Those of us who live in Baltimore City know what I'm talking about. Baltimore is like living in hell. Most of our killings that are committed, from what I can see, are really drug related murders in at least some sort of way. You see, there's three types of niggas in Baltimore. First, you got the *stick up niggas* who are just out to get some cash. Some fast money. Niggas who are basically, tired of being broke and simply just want what you go. It's that simple. How you get murdered is when you don't give up whatever it is that they want. Although, sometimes, you can still be shot even if you comply because you *are* able to identify them and that wouldn't be good for them now would it? Their victims usually consist of innocent, everyday people, or drug dealers. Secondly, you got the *niggas who are fighting over drug turfs*. To be real, Baltimore drug epidemic isn't nothing to sneeze at. It's like that for a reason. There's money to be made in Baltimore because of the extreme high rate of heroin addicts, cocaine addicts, and whatever drug of choice that interest you. You name it. So obviously, it's kind of safe to say that niggas are at least making a little change in Baltimore. When you're young, broke, raised up wrong in the first place, and you see no other *real* options to make some *real* money, what other choice do you see? That's the mentality of these types of niggas out here in Baltimore. They are willing, fully able, with a *nothing to lose attitude* to protect what is there's at all or any cost. Their victims can range from other drug dealers to innocent kids who are just in the wrong place at the wrong time. These niggas only see green, not red, and don't give a fuck period about life. Thirdly, you got the *junkies* who are addicted to the drugs that come from the second group mentioned. These type of niggas are sort of similar to the first group mentioned but there is a major difference. This group usually are so high, zooted, fucked up, whatever you want to call it, that they zap out, can't remember zapping out, and visions turn into nightmares. They are the type of niggas who will kill for a hit or something you got that they can sell for a hit. Their victims vary from complete strangers to family members with money. This type of drama unfolds every single day in Baltmore. Most of it doesn't even make the papers or the news because it's so common.

Understand that the drug problem is so out of control that you better school him or her about drugs while they are young because the attitude out here is, you've *never* smoked weed before? Or you've *never* sniffed coke before? It's almost unusual if somebody in your family is not addicted to some drug. *Seriously.* It's like, either you know somebody who is addicted to drugs or *you are* addicted to drugs. And, oh yeah, by the way, it's like that with our AIDS problem, too. Almost everybody I know has lost someone they loved to AIDS in Baltimore.

It's like everybody is either chasing some drug or
know somebody else who is chasing some drug. In
Baltimore, it's easier to get drugs than alcohol. Even
in the "good neighborhoods" of Baltimore City such as
the Inner Harbor or the condos in Fells Point, you can
still go within a mile radius and get drugs. Any kind
you want. All you have to do is cross Martin Luther
King Jr. Boulevard. Or even the East Side of
Hamilton. All you have to do is cross Loch Raven
Boulevard. Let's not even mention the schools.
My father's murder didn't even make the newspapers.
He was the forty sixth murder committed in 1995 and
it was only February. Homicide detectives were kept
so busy, that my mother was never even questioned.
Nobody was. Not even once. No matter how many
times I implicated her, she was never even considered.
They always claimed that they didn't have the
jurisdiction to travel all the way to North Carolina to
question her. They said they did not have probable
cause. I heard this over and over from every single
detective that handled this case. Once I was told that
the case file was misplaced somewhere. It was almost
as if his murder was meant to happen, because
whomever committed it, completely got away with it.
I was desperate to try anything, do anything, to put this
behind me and get to the truth once and for all.
I had an idea. For seven years I had prayed that I
could find out if my mother and brother was involved
in his murder. Now I finally came up with an idea that
I wasn't sure was going to work. I had nothing to lose
and only my sanity to gain.
I drove to a payphone next to a drug rehabilitation
center in Northwest Baltimore. I called the cold case

squad that was handling my father's case. I disguised my voice as I explained that I was calling about a murder that was committed in 1995. I told them that I was the girlfriend of one of the persons who committed this crime. I told them that I was dying of Aids and I wanted to clear my conscious before I died. I told them that the murder was committed by a friend of my then boyfriend. I was only on the phone for a few minutes but after I was done, I had certainly planted some seeds of doubt in the detectives mind. *Now something will get done, I thought.*

A few days later, the detectives called me to find out the name of any of my brother's girlfriends back in 1995. I gave them the name of the only one I knew about, and the only one I knew who would know something if he were involved. Within weeks, they located her. Homeless and addicted to crack cocaine, Monica finally confessed to the detectives what she knew. She admitted that his murder was planned by not only my brother and his friend, but she confessed that my mother knew as well. When the detectives related this to me by phone, I thanked them for their time.

Then I collapsed and dropped the phone.

They were jubilant about finally locating my mother and my brother and arresting them for this seven year old crime. Now they wanted to talk to me and find out everything I knew. I could hardly believe it when Sergeant Roland told me that Monica was confessing to everything. So it had been true all along. *I wasn't crazy,* I kept thinking. *I wasn't crazy.*

One week later, my mother and brother were arrested in North Carolina. They were brought home to

Baltimore by plane to face charges of first degree murder, conspiracy to commit murder, accessory to murder, solicitation to commit murder in the first degree. Later, my Mom calls me from the Baltimore City Detention Center and thanks me.

She says," I just want to thank you for this cause it's finally over. It has been hell for me for the past seven years."

I'm thinking, really?! It's been hell for you?!...

Chapter Nineteen

What I miss the most about Daddy is his sense of humor. He could always make me laugh. He was the funniest guy! All he did was crack jokes 24/7. He made a joke about us having the gas and electric off in the middle of hot ass August and we all laughed. He was so funny. I truly miss him on days when I yearn for a family. I think about him whenever I see an MTA bus. I think about how he walked, how he talked, how he loved music. I picture him in his MTA uniform and I miss him dearly. It's true that when somebody you love is no longer with you, you don't focus on the bad things that they did in life. You only think about the good times that you had with them. I never think about the drugs he did or the lifestyle that he led. You never know, he may have changed. Nobody is the judge of that. That was taken away from him by someone who had no right. I never got the chance to see if he would clean his life up, get sober. It was the one thing that I focused on when I called the detectives repeatedly. I wouldn't give up on finding out who did this to him no matter what the truth held.

Once I found out the truth, I began to rebuild my life. I imagined how my father would have wanted me to live my life. I completely kicked my weed habit from sheer will-power alone and began to hold myself accountable for my actions.

One of the first things I decided to do to get my life in order was to get in shape. I was an overweight, unhappy, weed-head with no goals in life. Slowly, I began getting back in shape. I started exercising, eating right, and handling stress the proper way instead of smoldering it with weed and sleeping pills. I got rid of all the negativity in my life, including the negative people that were walking all over me. Sometimes you have to walk away from all the negativity including people in your own family. I started planning for my future, which is something that I never even considered before. I always thought I would be dead before I reached twenty five. Now I wanted to live each day as an opportunity to do something that I had not done before. I saw each day as a challenge to do something with my life. I started praying to a God who I thought would help me. I developed my own personal relationship with God. It takes a lot of prayer to get out of anything that you are going through. That's the only way to make it out of the darkness. *The only way.* You have to believe that there is a higher power that can help you solve your problems. No matter how low you get, God is always there ready to lend a helping hand. I told myself that I had to look at life differently if I ever wanted to be happy. These choices were up to me and me alone to make. I had to get over the fact that we were not allowed friends. I had to stop blaming everybody for why I was always so shy and could never look anyone in the eye. I had to get over the problems that I faced as a child growing up. I told myself that after all I had been through, it would be a total waste if I decided to just do nothing with my life. What a complete waste. I felt I had no choice but to make something of myself.

By my thirtieth birthday, I had lost fifteen pounds and my self-esteem was better than it ever was before. I finally was able to look in a mirror and like what I saw. While my mother, my brother, and his friend Mark, sat in Baltimore City Jail awaiting trial, I began to finally put the past behind me. None of my other brothers and sisters could understand why I had chosen to continue to pursue his case. All they saw was that I was responsible for my mother and my brother being behind bars. I wasn't surprised when they all even stopped speaking to me. Both PJ. and my mother admitted that Mark had in fact killed him, but they both also denied any wrong doing. All three placed the blame on each other. Regardless of who did what, at least I now knew who his killers were. At least I had some sort of closure. At least I hadn't just forgotten about him like they wanted me to.

I began associating with my aunts, uncles, and cousins who were still viewed as enemies by my brothers and sisters. I was stunned when they welcomed me into their lives with open arms. All these years I had been told that they never cared about us, but they were determined to show me that that was never the case. I hadn't set eyes on any of them since I was a child and I was eager to establish some contact with at least somebody on my father's side. They all treated me

like a long, lost daughter. I finally had the "family
love" that I had been searching so long for.
If Daddy were alive today, there's no doubt in my
mind he would be proud of his daughter. I never gave
up pursuing his case and I think I turned out okay,
despite everything I've been through.
In fact, I'm sure he's laughing his ass off right now.

About the Author

Tia Lincoln, born and raised in Baltimore, Maryland is the owner of Old School/New School, a mobile disc jockey service. She resides in Baltimore with her husband, daughter, and son.